Table of Contents

Dedication

to friends

In the 1960s, my joyless introduction to sewing was the construction of a gingham apron, by hand, in a school Domestic Science lesson. I recall quiet, disciplined periods, painstaking attempts to sew less-than-perfect stitches, slow and silent shuffles in orderly lines toward the teacher for constructive criticism, and the inevitable unpicking that followed. These experiences were shared by my life-long friend, Janet Howson, the quiet initiator of all the mischief for which I was punished!

to teachers

As an accomplished quiltmaker, I have never forgotten that I was once a beginner. Jenny Dove started me on my quiltmaking journey in 1983, and I traveled through the learning maze over the years, gathering as much knowledge as possible about the many and varied techniques that come under the broad umbrella of quiltmaking. I have worked by hand and by machine and have loved every stitch of the journey!

to students

As an experienced teacher, I have probably learned more than I ever wanted to know about quiltmaking so that I may pass on the information to my regular students. I have great faith in the old saying, "If I hear, I forget. If I see, I remember. If I do, I understand," and thus, I teach my students by demonstration and practical example. I also try to pass on my endless enthusiasm as I inform my students about traditional techniques and exciting, new developments.

Thank you to all my contributors: Dot Aellen, Loretta Bailey, Joan Benton, Jo Butler, Bridget Coddington, Alexis Cowie, Freda Dodd, Connie Evans, Brenda Farnhill, Audrey Foster, Valerie Frazer, Jane Hadfield, Barbara Lane, Kath Lloyd, Pam Lloyd, Carole Mitson, Dorothy Morgan, Kath Norman, Liz Pedley, Margaret Robson, Joyce Seaton, Beth Stephenson, Ethelwyn Taylor, Gwenda Taylor, Gwyneth Thomas, Jenny Thomas, and Mary Williams.

And special thanks to Brian Pollard for his quiet professionalism and excellent photography.

to families

As one of the family, I have often needed a best friend, an ever-cheery helper, and a constant supporter—Roger has been all of those. I have also needed friendship, laughter, and relaxation outside my world of quilts—and that has been provided by our daughters, Tamana and Tessa, and their best mates, Nik and Richard.

to C&T

As an established writer, I am delighted to team up again with the expertise and magic of C&T to bring this book to you. They have assisted me in my endeavor to present this workshop book to you so that I may teach you in a clear and sympathetic way through its pages, as though I am sitting beside you as you sew. I would specifically like to acknowledge and thank my own wonderful team: Jan Grigsby, Cyndy Lyle Rymer, Rene Steinpress, Kristy Zacharias, and Matt Allen.

to you

Work your way through the straightforward four-step methods, and enjoy the informed and colorful journey through the workshops and projects. Absorb the tips, and be inspired by the student work and developmental ideas. But above all, ENJOY!

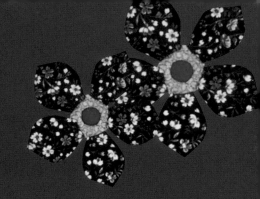

Introduction

Doily Art, 54″ x 54″, 1989, hand reverse appliquéd and hand quilted. A paper doily inspired my first reverse appliqué quilt

THIS BOOK IS FOR YOU!

The aim of this book is to teach hand and machine appliqué without the use of templates and it has developed as a direct result of my teaching experiences. It is a workshop book through which I can hopefully share my enjoyment of, and enthusiasm for, these specific methods of appliqué.

It contains patterns drawn to size where possible, step-by-step instructions, clear illustrations and, best of all, advice, however trivial, which only years of teaching can bring.

This book is ideal for the beginner who wants to learn how to sew accurate and safe appliqué without templates, by both hand and machine. From simple workshop beginnings, there is room for student development through the appealing floral projects.

It is also perfect for the more experienced sewer, offering original, inspirational and stimulating projects. Teachers are sure to find it an excellent resource book because it is laid out in workshop format. Whoever you are, this book is definitely for you!

- The beginner's workshops follow a regular format, using a standard 9″ square sample, to take you step-by-step, by text and illustration, through both the hand and machine methods of template-free appliqué.

- The easy-to-follow 4-step methods are not complex and the resulting appliqué shapes are as accurate as the drawn pattern line.

- The basic skills, learned in the workshops, are developed through a range of appealing projects which provide the opportunity to understand through practice.

- The projects, which explore and develop a variety of applications for the template-free applique methods, are inspiring and original.

- Each of the projects is associated with a particular workshop method, but they are also adaptable so the machine-sewn patterns can be tried by hand and the hand patterns by machine.

- The workshop methods can be adapted to any of your favorite appliqué patterns as long as a Master Pattern is available.

FROM NONSEWER TO "DILYS THE QUILT"

In 1983, when living in the south of England, I attended my first series of quiltmaking classes after responding to the harmless question, "Why don't you come along and have a go?" I couldn't believe the fascinating world I had stepped into; it was as though I had found where I wanted to be, without realizing that I had been searching for somewhere to go!

As a nonsewer, I had to learn the hard way. For example, when Jenny Dove, my teacher, told me that the way to get flat appliqué was to keep the fabrics as flat as possible, I took her literally, and I sewed my appliqué flat on a tabletop. I still do it this way.

I made my first quilt using templates. I traced the appliqué shapes, stuck the tracings onto cardboard, and then cut them out. I stored the templates for each pattern in envelopes, accompanied by a diagram to show the layout. This was the way I was taught to do it, and, at that time, it suited me fine.

It was when we moved to North Wales, in 1986, that I first heard about the UK National Patchwork Championships. I honestly believed that, to enter, I had to design my own quilt, no mean feat considering I had been told at school that I was useless at art. There were two certainties about this proposed competition quilt—it had to be an appliqué quilt, because that was all I could do, and it had to be made in smaller sections that would be quilted first before I began sewing it together.

Inspiration came during a visit to my parent's home. I started "to feel a quilt coming on" as I looked at my mother's Jacobean or crewelwork. And thus, *Jacobean Spring* was born. I worked on this quilt so intensively over a ten-week period that I loathed the sight of it when it was finished. I hastily sent it off, with relief, to the National Patchwork Championships, unwanted, unloved, and uninsured. Imagine my surprise when it won Best of Show and how carefully and respectfully I had it transported home!

The pressure was on to produce another quilt to affirm my place as a quilter. My ribbon-winning quilt, *Goodbye Crewel World*, followed two years later, and it represented another milestone in my development. It was the first time I had sewn the quilt top together before quilting.

Without these boosts to my confidence at the start of my quiltmaking journey, I might never have realized that I possessed a creative bone in my body, or a feel for color, or an aptitude for design. I had established a reputation with my first competition quilts and really needed to learn how to live and sew up to it! I studied new quiltmaking techniques from books and magazines and reinforced them in my skills vocabulary

Goodbye Crewel World, 70″ × 90″, 1988, hand appliquéd and hand quilted, with Italian quilting to emphasize the border pattern. This quilt was inspired by an antique crewelwork wallhanging made at the Lees Brother's factory in Birkenhead, Merseyside, UK. This factory, long since closed, trained young girls to make exotic wallhangings and sumptuous tapestries, which were then exported all over the world.

Jacobean Spring, 62″ × 78″, 1986, hand appliquéd and hand quilted. This quilt, my first competition entry, won Best of Show in the National Patchwork Championships in the United Kingdom. I simplified the Jacobean motifs to make sewing easier. The panels, which I sewed separately, reflect the nature of the Jacobean style of embroidery, in which a stem rises from the ground and throws out exotic flowers and leaves as it moves up the fabric.

through teaching. I always remained open-minded to new ideas, and I registered and developed my own preferences for color, style, and technique. It was with this attitude that I developed my innovative hand template-free method of appliqué fourteen years ago.

The moral of my quiltmaking journey is that if I can do it, anyone can. During the past twenty years, I have sewn whenever possible, taught extensively, written periodically, and never tired of it. There is a quaint tradition in Wales that trades people are often known locally as "Jones the Post," "Thomas the Milk," and so on. Since living in North Wales, where I have become acquainted with others who share the Welsh name of Dilys, I am often distinguished from them as "Dilys the Quilt"—a label I wear with pride.

Come join me on this floral journey into template-free appliqué by hand and machine. Learning the hard way has made me a sympathetic teacher; I hope this is evident throughout the book. You can learn the step-by-step methods through small workshop samples, which have lots of visual references. This book offers interesting and varied projects of increasing levels of difficulty to help you gain experience and develop the techniques, until you are as enthusiastic as I am about these accurate and reliable methods of doing appliqué, by hand and machine, without templates.

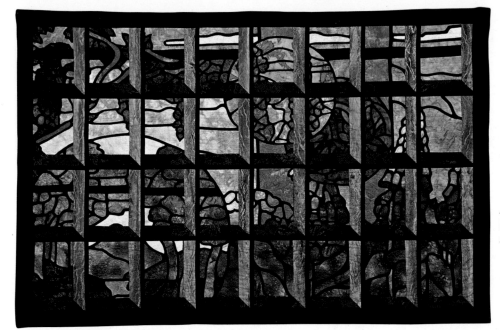

A Tiffany in the Attic, 58″ × 38″, 2003, hand reverse appliquéd, machine pieced, and machine quilted

APPLIQUÉ: A BRIEF HISTORY

There are many accounts of the history and development of appliqué in quiltmaking. Appliqué could be described as one of the earliest forms of patchwork because, functionally, it was used to patch a tear in a garment. It, therefore, has the humblest of roots. The need for thrift meant that clothes had to be repaired; the patching developed as a decorative feature. Eventually, appliqué was used alongside embroidery where rich and rare fabrics were used with expensive silks in such projects as ecclesiastical embroidery, banners, military clothing, and fabric ornamentation in castles and palaces.

In America, appliqué quilts first began to appear in about the 1750s. These quilts were always held in high esteem because of the time and expertise required to make them. As their appeal spread, the pioneer woman would probably have had two quilts on the go—the utility patchwork quilt for time snatched during chores and the appliqué quilt for when she was relaxed and unhurried and the light was good enough for fine work.

Appliqué is increasing in popularity today because it does not require the precision of fitting geometric shapes together, and the designs are often much freer and softer.

WHAT IS APPLIQUÉ?

Appliqué may be defined as the process of applying smaller fabric shapes onto a larger piece of fabric by hand or machine. If the shapes are appliquéd on top of a background fabric, the process is referred to as *positive appliqué*. If the edges of the shapes are appliquéd onto fabrics placed underneath, the process is called *negative* or *reverse appliqué*. Both types of appliqué can be done without templates.

DEVELOPING THE TEMPLATE-FREE METHODS

I have been using a template-free approach to my hand appliqué for many years, teaching it regularly in the United Kingdom and writing about it in books and magazines. But way back in 1984, when I was a beginner, I was taught to do hand appliqué with templates, preparing and basting the fabric shapes before positioning them onto the background fabric. I then learned how to do hand reverse appliqué with a needle-turn method, and I discovered that I loved the process of using the needle to control and sculpt the edges of the fabric shapes to the marked pattern line. This perhaps explains why I used a hand reverse appliqué technique to create many of my early quilts.

At the end of the 1980s, British textile artist Linda Straw wrote an article in a UK magazine about her award-winning, machine-appliquéd wallhangings. She described how she marked her pattern on the back of a foundation fabric and sewed along these lines from the back to machine baste the fabrics in sequence on the front. She pointed out that the lines sewn from the back showed the same on the front, but the shapes were reversed. This obvious but simple fact was a revelation to a hand sewer like me, who couldn't confidently sew more than a straight line by machine at that stage.

I began to think about working from the reverse by hand, and after several "what ifs" and many trials and errors, my hand method developed. My competency on the sewing machine also increased over the years, through necessity and dogged determination, giving me valuable practical experience and extensive knowledge of many machine appliqué methods. The methods that gave me, and therefore my students, the best results are detailed alongside my hand methods, forming the foundation of this book.

Tiffany Revisited, 58″ × 76″, 2003. This quilt was machine appliquéd, using commercially prepared bias binding and machine quilted.

THE ADVANTAGES OF THE TEMPLATE-FREE METHODS

◆ The methods require no templates, thus eliminating what can be a tedious stage in preparing appliqué shapes.

◆ The only preparation before basting is to transfer the master pattern onto a foundation or a background layer.

◆ The appliqué shapes are as accurate as the drawn pattern lines and are suitable for the novice, as well as the more experienced, sewer.

◆ The preparation methods result in fabric pieces being held securely onto the right side with either small hand-basted stitches or a machine-sewn line.

◆ Because there is little chance of the appliqué shapes moving during sewing, the method is tailor-made for those who need to pick up their work when they sew and who find it difficult to sew on a flat surface.

◆ The hand method is very portable, requiring little equipment.

Park Gates, 72″ × 67″, 2003. The machine-sewn background of squares is made up of fabric strips, machine quilted, and hand reverse appliquéd.

Christmas Rose, 32″ × 44″, 1992, hand and machine quilted. This quilt has a hand appliquéd center with a machine foundation pieced border.

Chapter One
Sewing Essentials

Hoffman Challenge, 25″ × 29″, 1994, hand reverse appliquéd and machine quilted

The basic supplies, listed in the first part of this chapter, are already available to all quilters, because I believe that the process of sewing should remain simple and uncluttered. The emphasis should be on the fabrics and on the sewing methods that will ultimately give the desired results. Pioneer women made some wonderful appliqué quilts with very few supplies to distract them. They made do with what was on hand.

The second part of the chapter explains and illustrates the basic skills required to help you make the workshop samples and the projects that follow. Concise instructions and clear illustrations, plus useful tips, make each process easy to understand. Tips are given for coping, by hand and machine, with concave and convex curves and for inward and outward points. I also explain my tabletop method of sewing, with details of the advantages of sewing this way.

The final part of this chapter details the techniques required to construct and finish the projects shown in the book, offering helpful advice on many skills, including straight and mitered borders, prairie points, bias preparation, and so on.

Supplies

BALLPOINT PEN Use with dressmaker's carbon paper to transfer the pattern onto dark fabric. The fine metal tip produces a clear line, and you can hold the pen efficiently to provide prolonged pressure. A dried up ballpoint pen provides the necessary pressure without smearing the pattern with ink.

BASIC SEWING SUPPLIES Straight pins, safety pins, sewing needles, and a thimble (optional).

BATTING A good-quality cotton batting stabilizes the fabric during quilting and assists with the drape of a wall quilt. I recommend a low-loft batting for the machine methods.

CUTTING BOARD, ROTARY CUTTER, AND RULER Use for cutting fabric squares, strips, and bias strips and for squaring the edges of pillows, wall-hangings, and quilts.

DRESSMAKER'S CARBON (TRACING) PAPER Recommended for transferring pattern lines onto dark fabric. Choose the white and yellow sheets to provide good, clear lines that remain visible during the sewing process.

FABRIC Use lightweight, good-quality cotton fabrics, prewashed at your own discretion.

FREEZER PAPER Use to transfer the pattern and to stabilize the fabric during machine stitching.

FUSIBLE WEB Use to bond fabrics together quickly and accurately, simply by ironing. Always follow the manufacturer's instructions.

MARKERS Available in the form of pencils, pens, chalk, soapstone, and so on. The aim is to find a suitable marker that remains clear for the length of time you are working on the fabric, but that fades or rubs off afterward. Test the marker on your fabric first, and follow the manufacturer's instructions.

MASKING TAPE Use to secure the pattern and fabric onto a flat surface.

SCISSORS Small scissors, with a sharp point, are essential for clipping seam allowances and cutting between the layers.

SEWING MACHINE IN GOOD WORKING ORDER Use for sewing seams, machine quilting and zigzag stitching, and assembling the projects.

THREAD For hand sewing, use good-quality cotton or silk threads that closely match the foreground fabrics. For machine sewing, use cotton or rayon threads. Use neutral threads for machine construction. You will also need threads for basting and for hand or machine quilting.

You may consider using invisible thread to machine appliqué in the bias method. It can also be used on the bobbin to machine baste fabrics of different colors.

STITCHING BASICS

Fabric Grains

The selvages, which are the finished edges of the fabric, are more tightly woven than the rest of the fabric. Remove selvages before using the fabric for any sewing project.

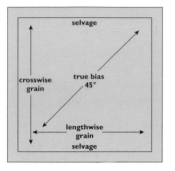

The lengthwise grain runs parallel to the selvage and has no stretch. The crosswise grain runs at right angles to the selvage and has a slight stretch. The bias runs at 45° to the selvage and has maximum stretch.

Needle-Turn Appliqué

This method of sewing is ideal for appliqué, as well as for reverse appliqué, because it provides accurately turned edges. Preparation is minimal, requiring only the transfer of a master pattern onto the fabric, a small amount of basting, and no templates. As the name suggests, you use the needle to turn under the seam allowance before sewing it down. With practice, you'll find that the needle becomes a valuable tool for maneuvering the seam allowance and establishing the edge of the shape by adjusting it. In both appliqué and reverse appliqué, you can rely on the same techniques to handle concave

and convex curves, outward points, and inward "V" shapes.

Being right-handed, I always sew counterclockwise (from right to left) around the outer edge of an appliqué shape. When sewing a reverse appliqué cutout, I still sew from right to left, but I sew in a clockwise direction, because I am sewing the inside edge. In either case, I work with the marked line closer to me than the cut edge of the fabric, because I find it more effective to sweep the seam toward me than to push it away. It is also easier to control the stitch and position the needle to catch the edge of the shape.

The Hand-Appliqué Stitch

Thread a needle with a color of thread that closely matches the foreground fabric, keeping in mind that the smaller the needle, the better the control. Put a small knot in the cut end of the thread to provide a firm anchor. Hide the knot under the marked line by bringing the needle up through the foreground fabric on the inside edge of the marked line.

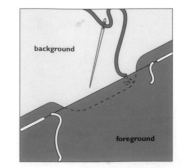

Anchor the knot under the folded edge.

Where possible, start to sew on a straight line or a gentle curve. Do not start at a point.

Stitch so the needle travels parallel to the edge and go straight down into the background fabric and slightly underneath the edge of the shape. Inserting the needle this way allows the thread to blend in better on the edge, concealing the stitch.

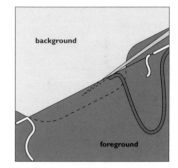

Insert the needle straight down into the background; take a small stitch.

Take a small stitch, about ⅛", in the background fabric and maneuver the needle back to the surface, catching the edge of the appliqué on the way up.

Longer stitches underneath result in gaps in the top stitches. These gaps allow the seam allowance to slip, resulting in corners on curves and loose ends on points.

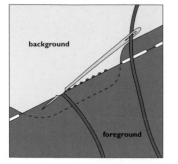

Guide the needle back up, catching the edge of the appliqué.

Make sure the thread comes out right on the edge of the fold for a concealed stitch.

The thread comes out on the edge of the fold.

Pull the sewing thread firmly to tighten the stitch but not so tightly as to cause puckering.

Continue sewing by inserting the needle into the background in the same place it came out. Remember that there is no forward movement on top; all the traveling must take place beneath the background fabric. Look at your stitches on the back. They should be small, traveling forward in a line and not at an angle, with no spaces in between

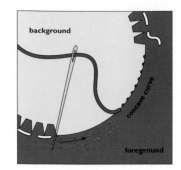

Test the seam by pulling at the edge of the appliqué shape. If you can see the stitches along the edge, you are either traveling forward with each stitch on top or not pulling your thread tight enough.

Sewing Curves

There are two types of curve—concave and convex—and they may range from gentle bends in a line to a tight inward or outward circle.

A **concave** curve "caves" or bows inward. With this curve, there will be less fabric at the cut edge of the seam allowance than at the marked edge of the shape. It is necessary to clip three-quarters of the way into the seam allowance to allow it to stretch as it is turned under.

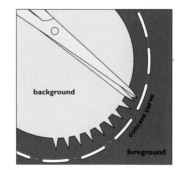

Clip three-quarters into the seam allowance on concave curves.

In general, the sharper the curve, the closer the clips should be. If the curve is severe, snip clips as close together as $1/8''$.

Use the needle to sweep under the seam allowance. Sew small, close stitches to secure the edge onto the

background fabric and to maintain the curve.

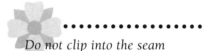

Sweep under the seam allowance.

A **convex** curve bows outward. With this curve, there will be more fabric at the cut edge of the seam allowance than at the marked edge of the shape. In this instance, use the needle to rearrange the seam allowance so it lies flat under the edge of the shape. These curves are often only as good as the marked line, so carefully transfer the pattern onto the fabric.

Do not clip into the seam allowances on convex curves, as this may encourage "corners" to appear on the sewn edge.

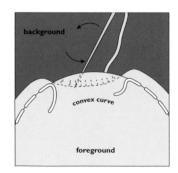

Sweep under the seam allowance to the marked line.

Using the tip of the needle, turn under and even out the seam allowance. Sew down the edge of the shape with small, close stitches to prevent the seam allowance from escaping. Turn and hold down only a small portion of the seam allowance at any one time, and sew a couple of close stitches before readjusting the seam to the marked line. On the edge of a circle, particularly a small one, take only one stitch at a time before readjusting.

Close stitching and constant readjustment to the line result in smooth convex curves.

If you turn under too much seam allowance and distort the edge of the shape, use the needle under the folded edge to ease the edge out to the marked line again.

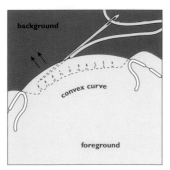

Use a needle to ease the shape.

Sewing the outward points

Outward points can vary from a gently angled corner to the sharpest of elongated points. Gentle points are easy to shape by sewing an extra stitch on the corner to hold the point. As the point sharpens, however, the space where the fabric has to be folded becomes smaller. For that reason, you may need to trim some of the excess fabric.

As you approach the point, bring the stitches closer together and sew right to the tip. Add an extra stitch on the point to anchor it.

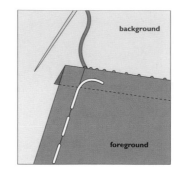

Bring the stitches closer.

Rotate the background fabric so that the seams on the point lie to the side.

Pick up both seam allowances and sweep the point of the needle toward yourself, so the seam allowances fold under the shape and lie against the stitched edge.

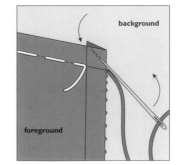

Pick up the seam allowances near the fold; sweep under.

Holding the point down, tug on the stitch at the point to sharpen it. Sew close stitches on the other side of the point to hold under the seam allowance.

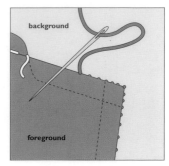

Add an extra stitch on the point, sew away along the next side.

If the point is elongated and there is too much fabric in the seam allowance to hide underneath, reduce the fabric bulk. As before, anchor the point with an extra stitch and then fold back the appliqué shape to reveal the turned seam allowance under the point. Using sharp scissors, cut parallel to the direction of the point, trimming away a small amount of the fabric in the seam allowance. Turn under the remaining seam allowance, hold down the fabric on the point, and use the needle to readjust the seam allowance so it lies flat. Sew away from the point with close stitches, as before.

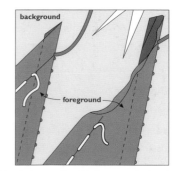

Fold back the appliquéd shape and trim the excess fabric.

Sewing the inward V shapes

At the point of the V, the seam allowances go in opposite directions, leaving no fabric to turn under. Because the stitches here will always be visible, a good match of thread with fabric is important.

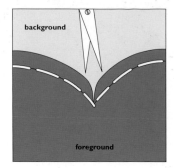

Clip the V.

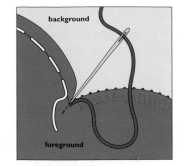

Stitch close to the V. Bring the needle up deep into the V.

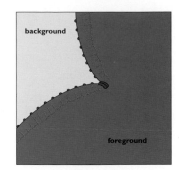

Take a stitch into background. Sew away from the V.

Clip to the marked line at the V, but do not cut thruogh the line. Sweep under the seam allowance with the needle. Maintain the shape by sewing with close stitches.

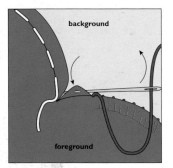

Sweep under the seam allowance.

As you approach the V, bring the stitches on the turned edge closer together, slightly less than $1/8$" apart. Sew to within $1/8$" of the inward point, taking care to avoid fraying the edge. Insert the needle down into the background fabric, as if you were making a stitch, but bring it up $1/8$" below the marked point of the V. There is nothing to turn under here, so you need to bind the threads in the V.

Be aware that V shapes cut on the bias of the fabric do not fray as readily as those cut on the grain of the fabric.

Take a stitch into the foreground fabric only, to come up in the same place and pull it deep into the V. Sew a second stitch in the same way to bind the threads.

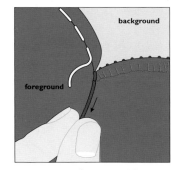

Take a stitch through foreground fabric only. Pull to tighten.

Pull tight on these binding stitches and take another stitch deep into the V through the background fabric, securing the shape in place. Rotate the shape, turn the seam allowance under on the other side of the V, and sew away from the V with close stitches.

Finishing

Take the needle through to the wrong side of the work. The appliqué shapes are clearly defined by small stitches. Make two small, tight stitches just inside the sewn line to finish, and clip the thread.

The Tabletop Method of Hand Appliqué

My tabletop hand-sewing procedure began as a misunderstanding between my teacher and me. Not being a natural sewer, I had to learn the hard way as I initially struggled for results and eventually for excellence. My teacher told us that our goal was to produce flat appliqué. To do this, we had to keep our fabrics as flat as possible while we were sewing. I took her literally, and started to sew, trying to keep my fabrics flat on the table. Although this initially proved awkward and often frustrating, I persevered until it became second nature.

If you wish to try this method, remember that it gets easier with practice! I sew on a tray that has a bag of small polystyrene balls attached underneath. I place the area to be worked so it is centered on the tray, and I safety pin the surrounding fabric onto the sides of the bag. This keeps the work flat and secure, and I can tilt the board at an angle to give a more relaxed sewing position.

Sewing on a tilted board

Close up of position of the hands and the needle

Sewing using the tabletop method

Your right hand controls the needle and your left hand is on top of the work, with the fingers along the edge of the line to be sewn. (Reverse this arrangement if you are left-handed.) Your right thumb and forefinger direct the needle into the fabric. Your middle finger, thimbled for protection if preferred, pushes the needle through, to be collected again by the thumb and forefinger.

The fingers of your left hand act as a buffer at the edge of the shape. As the needle negotiates the fabric, your fingers prevent the edge from slipping. Push the edge of the shape against your index finger, allowing the needle to catch the underside of the fold on its way up again.

The Machine Appliqué Stitch

The purpose of the zigzag stitch is to cover the basting stitches and to prevent the edges of the fabric from fraying. For this stitch to be effective, most of it should lie on the appliqué shape, with the outward swing entering the background fabric right up to the edge of the shape. If the edge of the appliqué shape is not fused, the zigzag stitches need to be very close; this is known as *satin stitch*. If the edge is fused, the fabric threads are bonded together, and the zigzag stitches can be spaced out. Test the stitch on your machine to give the look you require. I strongly recommend using an open-toe appliqué foot, as it allows you to see exactly where the needle is in relation to the edge of the appliqué.

• • • • • • • • • • • • • • • • • •

Prepare a batting sandwich, and sew lines of zigzag stitches of varying widths and densities. With a permanent marker, note the settings beside the lines, and keep this by your machine for reference.

The thread for machine appliqué can match the fabric to blend into the edge of the shape, or it can contrast with the fabric to define the edge more strongly. For good tension, use the same sewing thread, or a finer thread, in your bobbin. Machine appliqué is sewn in sequence, from background to foreground, just like hand appliqué.

There are several advantages to the tabletop method.

• The fabrics remain flat and do not move in relation to one another. There is none of the distortion that sometimes occurs when your fingers are underneath the fabrics.

• The table supports your elbows, eliminating the strain in the upper arm and neck region. A tilted board underneath the work area stops you from hunching over your sewing.

• It is often easier to see the design more fully when it is in front of you rather than when it is in your lap. This makes it easier to see the shapes in relation to each other and to assess your progress during sewing.

• Although most of the sewing occurs alongside the index finger, you can hold down longer sections of seam allowance, using the rest of your fingers on top of the work.

• Extensive basting is unnecessary, which must be an advantage! I often use small safety pins in my work, eliminating basting altogether.

• This technique is adaptable to any room in your home: place a tray across the arms of the chair to create a work surface at a comfortable height, and use a daylight bulb in a well-placed lamp for good lighting.

Preparing to sew

Set the machine to sew a straight stitch, and start sewing on a straight or slightly curved edge.

To prevent tangled threads on the back of a project, get into the habit of doing the following simple maneuver at the start of a machine-sewn line.

Line up the needle with the edge of the appliqué, and drop the foot onto the fabric to engage the stitch. Hold onto the top thread, without adding tension, and sew a single stitch into the background fabric, right up to the edge of the appliqué.

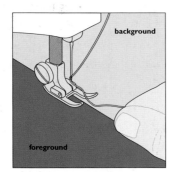

Hold thread without tension for one stitch.

Lift the foot, and pull the fabric toward you on the sewing table. Tug on the top thread to pull the bobbin thread onto the top of the work.

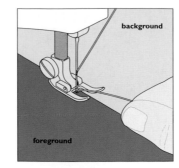

Tug the top thread.

Reposition the fabric under the foot, and ease the needle into the same hole at the edge of the shape. Put the presser foot down again to grip the fabric, so it is ready for sewing.

Starting to sew

In the explanations that follow, the "zig" part of my stitch swings to my left and the "zag" part to my right as I am facing my machine. I always machine sew clockwise around the edges of the appliqué shapes and counterclockwise around reverse appliqué holes. In other words, my appliqué shape is always to the left of the needle and the background is always on the right.

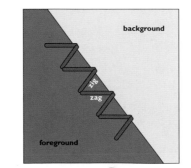

Zig to the left, zag to the right.

Adjust the straight stitch length so you get about six tiny stitches per $1/4''$, and sew these straight stitches into the background fabric along the edge of the shape. With the needle out of the fabric, set the machine to sew the width and density of the zigzag stitch you require.

Be aware that the zigzag stitch swings the same distance on each side of the needle. Adjust the position of the foot so that the "zig" swing goes onto the appliqué shape and the "zag" finishes in the background fabric, right at the edge of the shape. Work in a controlled way around the edge, sewing around the changes in the shape, as follows.

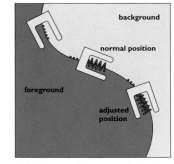

Position the foot so that most of the zig zag stitch lies on the appliqué.

Sewing the curves

Because the machine only sews in a straight line, you have to adjust the position of the fabric to help the machine change direction. These adjustments are made on the side of the zigzag stitch that has to travel the longest distance, with the general rule that the tighter the curve, the more the stitch needs to be adjusted.

CONCAVE CURVES The distance is shorter at the edge of the fabric shape. Make adjustments when the needle is down in the appliqué shape (after the "zig" swing). Make more adjustments on a tighter curve.

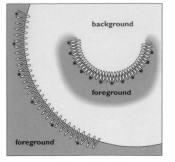

Adjust direction of the stitch with needle down in foreground fabric.

CONVEX CURVES

CONVEX CURVES The distance at the edge of the shape is longer. Make adjustments when the needle is down in the background fabric (after the "zag" swing). Again, make more adjustments on a tighter curve.

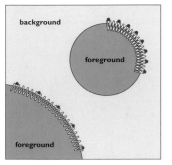

Adjust direction of stitch with needle down in background fabric.

Sewing the outward points

A RIGHT-ANGLED CORNER Sew to just beyond the corner, stopping after the "zag" swing with the needle down in the background fabric. The following "zig" will swing to the left. Rotate the project 90° so that it swings on top of the stitches that you have just sewn. Continue sewing away from the corner.

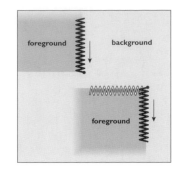

Rotate on outer swing with needle down in background fabric.

AN ELONGATED POINT When sewing a sharp point, the needle eventually starts to swing into the background fabric on both sides of the appliqué shape. Stop at this point with the needle down, and adjust the fabric so that the point is centered under the needle. Continue to sew slowly over the tip, reducing the width of the swing until there is no sideways movement at all. Leave the needle in the fabric at the point, and rotate the fabric 180°. As you start to sew again, gradually increase the width of the swing back to your chosen setting and continue to sew away from the point.

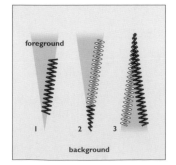

Reduce width of stitch toward point. Rotate at tip; increase width while sewing away from point.

Sewing the inward V shapes

Stop sewing when the needle is right in the V, with the needle down in the background fabric. Sew three com-

plete zigzag stitches into the V, holding onto the fabric so that that there is no forward movement. Sew one stitch at a time, rotating the V after each stitch. Make sure that each "zag" goes into the same hole in the background fabric. Do one stitch just before the V, one directly on the V, and one just after, before sewing along the next side.

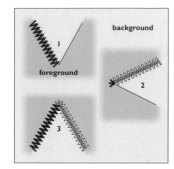

Sew a stitch before V, one on the V, and one after.

Finishing

When you get back to where you started, continue sewing the zigzag stitches over the top of the tiny starting stitches to cover them, if appropriate. When the zigzag stitches meet, adjust the machine to sew tiny straight stitches again. Reposition the shape under the foot so that the needle sews along the edge of the zigzag stitches that are on the appliqué shape. Sew six tiny stitches to complete the line.

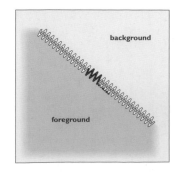

Sew back to start; finish with tiny stitches.

BASIC TECHNIQUES

Preparing a Master Pattern

Because book pages are limited in size, it is sometimes necessary to prepare a master pattern before starting a project. This is particularly true for the various template-free techniques that need a complete pattern to transfer onto the fabric.

1. Cut paper to the size of the piece of work stated in the pattern. Draw vertical and horizontal centerlines.

2. Make multiple tracings or photocopies of the pattern sections to the required size. Tape them to the paper, being aware of the centerlines.

Adding a Seam Insert

To define a seam or to emphasize a border strip, add a small, folded insert of contrasting fabric before sewing on the border strips.

1. Cut the contrasting fabric $3/4''$ wide by the length of the edge. Fold it in half, wrong sides together, and press.

2. With all raw edges even, baste the strip in place, using an $1/8''$ seam allowance and matching thread. When you sew the border with a $1/4''$ seam, you will see $1/8''$ of the insert.

Press wrong sides together; baste in place.

Adding Straight Borders

1. Measure the size of the square or rectangle (for example, $12^{1/2''} \times 12^{1/2''}$) and decide on the width of the border strips (for example, $3^{1/2''}$, which results in an $18^{1/2''} \times 18^{1/2''}$ square). Cut the top and bottom border strips as long as the top edge of the square and as wide as the border (for example, $12^{1/2''} \times 3^{1/2''}$).

2. Using a $1/4''$ seam, sew the edges in place (short strips first), and press both seam allowances toward the border.

Sew short strips before adding longer side strips.

3. Measure the center square from top to bottom, including the borders

(in my example, $18^{1/2''}$). Cut the strips this long and as wide as the border (or $18^{1/2''} \times 3^{1/2''}$).

4. Sew the strips to the sides of the square. Press the seams toward the border.

Adding Mitered Borders

1. Measure the size of the square (for example, $14^{1/2''} \times 14^{1/2''}$) and decide on the width of the border strips (for example, $2^{1/2''}$, which results in an $18^{1/2''} \times 18^{1/2''}$ square). Cut the strips long enough to allow the fabrics to overlap comfortably on the corners ($19^{1/2''} \times 2^{1/2''}$).

2. Using pins, mark the center of each side of the square and the center of each border strip.

3. Match the center points, and pin the borders to the square, with right sides together and raw edges even. An equal amount of border fabric will extend beyond each corner.

4. Starting and stopping $1/4''$ in from the corners, sew each border to the square. Backstitch to make the corners secure, and remove the pins. Press the seams toward the outside edge.

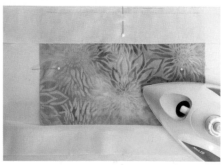

Center strip; start sewing $1/4''$ from a corner. Finish $1/4''$ from next corner.

Add side borders, leaving the corners free.

5. Carefully fold the center square diagonally, right sides together, lining up the border strips at the corners. Pin the strips to prevent them from slipping. Extend the diagonal line onto the border strips by drawing or creasing against a ruler.

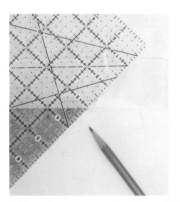

Fold center square on the diagonal; Extend diagonal line onto border strips.

6. Sew on this line by hand or machine, starting from the point on the corner where the previous stitches stopped. Trim away the excess fabric, leaving a ¼″ seam allowance.

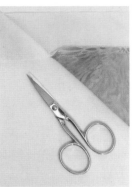

Pin and sew along marked line, trim excess fabric.

Repeat the procedure for each corner. Press the seams open.

Preparing Bias Tubes

Iron-on bias binding is now readily available in a variety of plain colors and shaded sequences, and it does save a lot of time. Simply iron the ready-fused tubes in place; you can then complete the whole pattern before sewing. A small travel iron is compact and easy to maneuver and makes the bias application easier. Iron-on bias binding is particularly good for large machine appliqué projects with simple lines.

Where intricate shaping is required, I recommend a prepared bias binding. You may use any cotton fabric to add an exciting and unique finish to a project, as seen in the sample for Workshop 5 (page 57). You may also choose to iron thin strips of fusible web to the back of prepared binding tubes, so that they can be fused in place for machine sewing.

Machine preparation

1. Cut several 1″ strips along the bias of the fabric. Fold the strip in half along its length, wrong sides together and raw edges even. Using a matching thread, sew ¼″ from the folded edge to make a tube. Trim the seam allowance to ⅛″, and slide the tube onto a ¼″ bias bar.

Most bias projects require tubes of varying lengths, so prepare all the strips cut from a square of fabric. Remember to use the shorter lengths where they fit and keep the longer lengths for longer pattern lines.

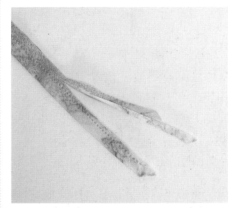

Sew bias strip ¼″ from folded edge; trim seam allowance to ⅛″.

It is easier to cut away a seam allowance after sewing than to handle a strip that is narrower than 1″.

2. Maneuver the seam to center it on the flat side of the bar, with the seam allowances going in the same direction. You may need to dampen your fingers to make maneuvering the seam easier.

3. Ease the end of the bias tube off the bar to trap it under the tip of an iron. Press both seams in the same direction as you ease the tube off the bar.

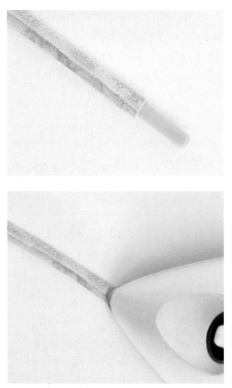

Center the seam; press to one side as it comes off the bar.

Hand preparation

1. Cut and prepare several ¾″ strips along the bias of the fabric. With the wrong side on the inside, make a tube by folding each strip into thirds along its length. Make sure that the raw edge does not extend beyond the folded edge.

2. Use a contrasting thread and small stitches to baste along the center of the tube. Press to sharpen the edges.

Intricate pattern shapes require thinner and more maneuverable tubes. Finer strips (⅝″ or ½″) can be prepared in this way.

Sewing the prepared bias tubes

1. Sew the bias tubes in numerical sequence, by hand or machine, to give the impression that the background shapes lie underneath those in the foreground. If the sewing sequence is not marked on the master pattern, you must figure it out before sewing.

2. Position the prepared tube along the selected pattern line, making sure it extends ½″ beyond the start and the finish. Secure it with pins that make a bridge over the tube.

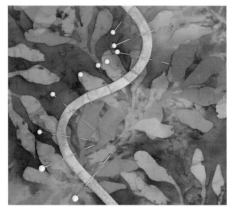

Pin to form a bridge over the bias tube.

Pinning into the thickness of the tubes can cause distortion. Insert the pins as close as possible to the binding, on both sides, so it can't move from side to side but it can be pulled under the pins. The more severe the curve, the closer the pins should be.

3. For hand sewing, baste along the line to secure and remove the pins. Using a matching thread and small, concealed stitches (page 13), appliqué the edges of the tube onto the fabric below.

4. Always sew along the shortest, or concave, edge first, where appropriate. Put a tuck in the point to change direction.

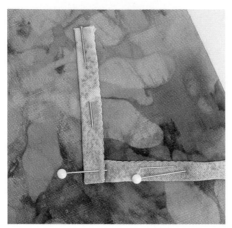

Put a tuck in point to change direction.

5. There is no need to baste for machine sewing. Select your stitch and remove the pins just ahead of the foot as you sew with a matching or invisible thread.

6. Sew the tubes using your preferred method.

Narrow zigzag · Blind stitch · Wide zigzag · Hand appliqué · Straight stitch

Sew the strips. (Note: Contrasting thread was used for greater visibility.)

7. After sewing, trim away the excess fabric at both ends of the tube so that the raw edge lies no more than ¹⁄₁₆″ beyond a crossing pattern line. Continue to position, sew, and trim the tubes in sequence, and press gently from the reverse to complete.

Making Continuous Prairie Points

Each prairie point will finish equal in size to one-quarter of the width of the fabric strip from which it is cut. For example, the points will be 2″ if you cut them from an 8″-wide strip.

1. Cut a strip of fabric the required width (for example, 6″), and press it in half along its length, wrong sides together. Open it again, and lay it on a flat surface, wrong side up, for marking and cutting.

2. Mark the centerline in the fold. Measure and mark each side of the centerline, dividing each section accurately into staggered or offset squares (for example, 3″). In other words, the corner of the square on one side will lie midway between the corners of the square on the other side.

3. Trim the unwanted half square (for example, 3″ × 1½″) at the beginning and end of each staggered line.

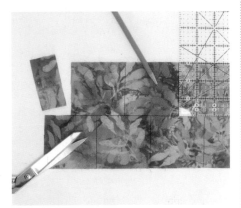

Mark and cut into sections; stagger sides.

4. Cut along the marked lines from the raw edge to the fold along the entire length of the strip.

5. Press each square in half on the diagonal to make triangles.

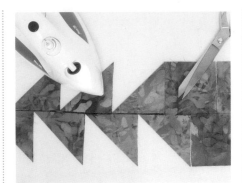

Press squares.

6. Fold each triangle in half again, making it smaller. The raw edges should meet along the fold of the strip. Fold the strip in half again lengthwise. Tuck the prairie points together, one into the next, and baste ⅛″ from the folded edge. Press.

Press in half again; fold 2 sides together.

Making an Overlapped Pillow Back

1. Measure the pillow front (for example, 18″), and cut 1 piece that is the same width and half the length plus 1″ for a seam allowance (for example, 18″ × 10″).

2. Turn under and stitch the seam allowance (so the pillow measures 18″ × 9″), and place the piece, wrong side up, on a flat surface.

3. Cut another piece that measures the width of the pillow and half the length plus 5″ (for example, 18″ × 14″).

4. Turn under and stitch the seam allowance so the pillow measures 18″ × 13″). Place and pin the larger piece, wrong side up, on top of the smaller piece, making a square the same size as the pillow front (for example, 18″).

5. Place the pillow front right side up on top, matching the raw edges. The pillow is now ready for binding.

For speed and to avoid binding, pin the prepared back to the pillow front, right sides together. Sew a ¼″ seam around the outside edge, and turn the pillow right sides out through the overlapped back.

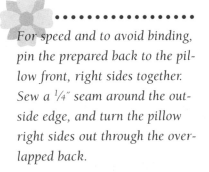

Prepare one piece half the size of pillow. Prepare a second piece 4″ larger. Overlap one piece on top of the other.

Making a Zippered Pillow Back

1. Measure the front of the pillow (for example, 16″), and cut a square of fabric that is 2″ larger (in this case, 18″). Cut the fabric square in half (18″ × 9″). On the wrong side of one half, draw a line 1″ from the cut edge.

2. Oversew the raw edges, and baste the pieces, right sides together, along the marked line. Press the seam from the wrong side.

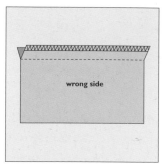

Baste pieces together.

3. Use a zipper that is 1″ shorter than the pillow front (for example, 15″). Hand-baste the zipper over the seam. Sew close to the teeth.

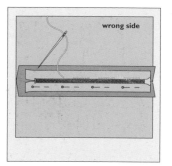

On wrong side, hand baste zipper over seam.

4. On the right side, machine sew outside the basting stitches. Remove the basting stitches to reveal the zipper.

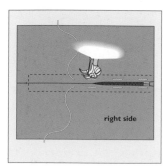

On right side, machine sew outside basting stitches.

5. Position the prepared pillow back so it is right side down on a flat surface. Place the pillow front on top, right side up and centered. Trim the excess fabric to even the edges. The pillow is ready for binding.

Using See-Through Rulers

The long, see-through rulers that you use with a rotary cutter and cutting board are invaluable in the finishing-off process. These transparent rulers allow you to line up the ruler's vertical and horizontal lines with the seams and the straight edges in your projects to make right-angled corners. You can also use the 45° diagonal lines to mark quilting lines and to angle the ends of wallhangings.

Use the square see-through rulers to estimate the size of the rectangles required for the template-free methods. Place the corner of the ruler over the motif, and note the actual measurements. Being aware of the fabric's straight of grain, use the ruler to cut out a rectangle that is ³⁄₄″ larger than the actual measurements. As you become more experienced, you can simply add ¹⁄₂″ to the actual measurements to save fabric.

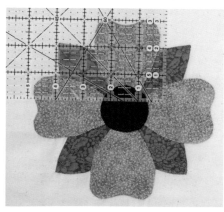

Use a square ruler to estimate size of fabric rectangles required for template-free methods.

Quilting

In addition to holding the layers of the quilt together, quilting adds texture to the overall design. Quilting close to an appliquéd edge (quilting in-the-ditch) allows the shape to fill out. Lines of quilting repeated around shapes (echo quilting) help emphasize shapes. Patterns and grids on the background help unify the different blocks in a quilt.

Transferring pattern lines for quilting

The marked line needs to be obvious during the quilting process, but it also needs to disappear into the line of stitches once it has been sewn.

1. Press the quilt top, and remove any loose threads from the back. This is particularly important if you are using a light background; "ghosts" of loose threads can appear and will be difficult to remove after quilting.

2. The easiest way to transfer a pattern onto a light fabric is to trace it; however, this is difficult with a dark fabric. For dark fabrics, place a light source beneath the pattern so you can see the lines clearly as you transfer them.

3. Place the marked top, right side up, onto the batting and backing, both of which should be cut slightly larger (in case of movement during quilting).

4. Pin the quilt layers together and then thread baste in horizontal and vertical rows spaced 3″–4″ apart. For machine quilting, use safety pins rather than basting thread.

Examples of Textural Machine Quilting

Whatever you can draw with a pencil, you should be able to draw with the machine needle! An acquired skill, free-motion quilting is useful when quilting a large quilt, the main advantage being that there is no need to rotate the quilt. For this technique, you need a good grip on the quilt for extra control. Aim for steady coordination of the sewing speed, regulated by your foot, and of the stitch length, controlled by your hand. I leave my feed dogs up for a bit of extra grip on the underside of the quilt. Remember that practice makes perfect.

Textured machine quilting with continuous lines

Spray basting adhesive can be used to combine the layers. Use the spray in a well-ventilated area, following the manufacturer's instructions.

Attaching a Hanging Sleeve

I automatically attach a hanging sleeve to the back of my quilts and wallhangings, matching the backing fabric to conceal the sleeve.

1. Cut a strip of backing fabric 4½″ wide and 1″ shorter than the measurement of the top edge of the quilt.

2. Turn under and sew a small seam on each short edge. Iron under a ¼″ seam along one long edge.

3. Pin the sleeve onto the back of the quilt, with the right side uppermost and the raw edges even.

4. Sew the top edge into the binding. Sew the lower edge to the backing layer by hand, using matching thread and concealed stitches.

If you prefer, you may protect the back of your quilt by using a double sleeve: Cut fabric 8½″ wide and 1″ shorter than the top edge. Narrowly hem the short edge, and fold the fabric in half, wrong sides together. Catch the long raw edges in the seam when binding the top edge of the quilt. Sew the folded edge of the sleeve to the backing fabric by hand.

Double-Fold Binding

Preparing a binding strip

1. Measure around the outside edge of the quilt or pillow front.

2. On the straight grain of the fabric, cut 2″-wide strips to exceed this measurement by 10″.

3. Stitch these strips together to make a single piece long enough to travel all the way around the edge and to give a generous overlap.

Use a diagonal (bias) seam to join the binding strips; this is better than a straight one because it adds less bulk to the seam.

4. To join with a diagonal seam, place 2 strips right sides together and at right angles to one another. Sew at a 45° angle, and cut away the excess fabric on the corner, leaving a ¼″ seam allowance.

5. Iron the seam open, and fold and press the strip in half along its length, wrong sides together.

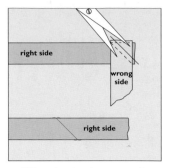

Sew at a 45° angle; trim the corner. Press seam open.

6. Cut the starting edge of the binding at a 45° angle to tidy the edge. Turn and press a ¼″ seam allowance.

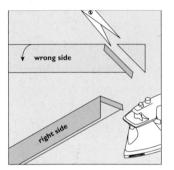

Start strip at an angle.

Binding the edges

Check that your binding strip is long enough to go all the way around the edge, adding an extra 10″ to allow for mitered corners and an overlap at the ends.

1. Place the start of the binding strip about 3″ from a corner, matching the raw edges of the strip with those of the pillow or quilt. Leaving about 2″ at the start for the overlap, sew on the binding with a ¼″ seam. Stop sewing ¼″ in from the corner, and backstitch to secure the stitches. Remove from under the sewing foot.

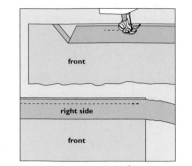

Start sewing 2″ from end. Stop ¼″ from corner.

2. Make a tuck on the corner by pulling the binding away from you at a 90° angle to the top of the pillow and then toward you again, so that the raw edges lie along the next side to be sewn. The fold of the tuck must be level with the raw edges of the pillow or quilt.

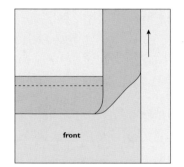

Pull binding away at corner.

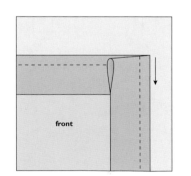

Pull binding toward you to make a tuck level with raw edge.

If the tuck is too low, the corner will be squashed; if the tuck is too high, the corner will be elongated.

Insert the corner under the sewing foot again. From the top of the tuck, resume sewing a ¼″ seam.

3. After sewing the final corner, trim the end of the binding to a 45° angle, to overlap the starting edge by ½″. Slide it inside the start of the strip and sew to complete the seam.

4. Turn the folded edge onto the back of the quilt. Hand sew it using matching thread and concealed stitches, mitering the extra fabric on the corners. Hand sew the overlapped seams.

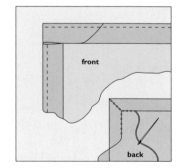

Overlap binding. Sew folded strip by hand on back.

Chapter Two

The Beginner's Workshops

his chapter introduces you to seven template-free methods in an easy-to-follow workshop format. Small practical samples guide you step by step through each method, offering helpful tips to make the process easy to understand and to practice. The sample squares all measure 9″ × 9″, so you can keep them on file for future reference or develop them as suggested. At the end of each workshop, specific projects help you practice and develop the skills you have learned.

In appliqué, be aware of the following:

◆ Background refers to the fabric onto which all the pattern shapes are appliquéd.

◆ Foreground refers to the fabric shapes that are appliquéd onto the background fabric.

In reverse appliqué, be aware of the following:

◆ Foreground refers to the fabric onto which the pattern is transferred and from which the pattern shapes are cut.

◆ Background refers to the fabrics placed underneath that will be visible through the cut shapes in the foreground fabric.

NOTE: I recommend using good-quality cotton fabrics for the workshops.

In the instructions that follow, please note that WS stands for wrong side and RS for right side.

Blue Hawaii, 42″ × 42″, 1993, hand appliquéd and hand quilted. This quilt was juried into the Fifth National Exhibition of the Quilters' Guild of the British Isles, "A New Look at Old Traditions."

Whether you are sewing patchwork blocks together or appliquéing shapes onto a background, remember that you are recreating a piece of fabric in which the straight grains should ideally run vertically and horizontally. In the workshops, you will be encouraged to prepare squares, strips, and rectangles of fabric for the foreground appliqués or the background reverse appliqués, so you can easily identify and position the grainlines.

Template-Free Method by Hand
Symmetrical Motif

This workshop provides a gentle introduction to the hand method. An easy pattern with simple lines is traced onto a light background fabric. The shapes are basted in sequence, and the excess fabric is cut away to leave a small seam allowance to be needle-turned. The pattern is not reversed on the right side.

FABRIC REQUIREMENTS

BACKGROUND
9″ × 9″ light fabric

FOREGROUND
4 squares 2¾″ × 2¾″ for leaves, 1 square 7½″ × 7½″ for petals, and 1 square 2½″ × 2½″ for center

OTHER SUPPLIES

THREADS that closely match the foreground fabrics

MASKING TAPE

WATER-SOLUBLE MARKER

BASIC SEWING SUPPLIES (see page 12)

PREPARATION

Transfer the pattern on page 31 onto a light background by tracing.
Study the master pattern to become familiar with the position and the
sewing sequence of the leaves, petals, and center. Find the centerlines of the
background fabric by folding and finger-pressing. Mark WS for wrong side
in one corner of the back of the fabric, and transfer the pattern and the
number sequence onto it. The unmarked side of the fabric is the right side,
onto which you will appliqué the shapes.

*If you use a water-soluble marker on light fabric, you can often see
the line on the right side. This can provide a useful guide when
needle-turning the edge of the shape.*

ASSEMBLY

1. **Place the shapes on the background fabric.** Work with the square of
leaf fabric for a #1 shape first. Place the fabric right side down on a flat surface. Place the background fabric on top, with the marked side uppermost.
(In other words, the wrong side of the leaf fabric should be against the right
side of the background fabric.) Make sure the sides of both squares are parallel to one another to match the fabric grains. The leaf fabric will be seen as
a shadow underneath the fabric, so make sure it covers the #1 shape with at
least ½″ to spare all round as a "comfort zone." Adjust if necessary, and pin
at the four corners to secure.

*After pinning from the wrong side, turn over the sample, and
reposition the pins on the right side so they do not catch the thread
during basting.*

2. **Baste the shapes onto the background fabric.** Working from the
wrong side, where the pattern lines are visible, use a thread that contrasts
with the appliqué fabric. Hand baste with small stitches *all around* the leaf
shape, sewing directly on the marked line. Be aware that some lines will be
overlapped by the petals and the center. It is helpful to distinguish these
lines by lengthening the basting stitches. Make sure the fabric on the right
side remains as flat as possible. Repeat to baste the remaining leaf shapes.

*Keep the stitches small and regular to define the shape accurately. In
general, the more intricate the shape, the smaller the stitches should be.*

3. **Trim the foreground shapes.** Turn over to the right side of the background fabric, where the leaf shapes are defined by the basting stitches. Use
small sharp scissors to trim the excess fabric from around each shape, leaving

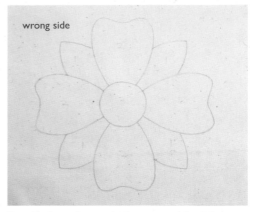

wrong side

Transfer the pattern onto the wrong side of the
background fabric.

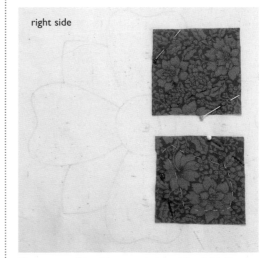

right side

Pin squares, right sides up, on right side of fabric.

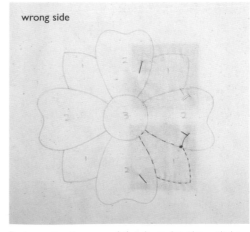

wrong side

Baste on the line around the shape; lengthen stitches
where shape will overlap.

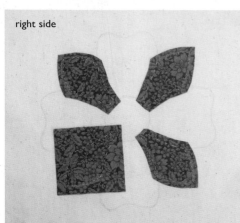

right side

Trim excess fabric.

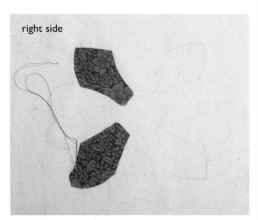

right side

Remove basting stitches; needle-turn the edge.

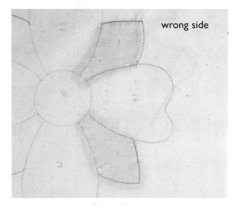

wrong side

Appliqué stitches follow line on the wrong side.

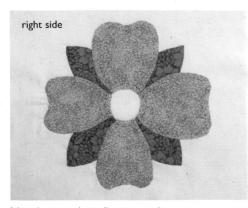

right side

Next baste and needle-turn petals.

four separate leaf shapes, each with a seam allowance of $^3/_{16}''$. Use a suitable marker to mark the edges that will be turned under on the outside edge of the basting stitches.

Marking is optional, because the stitches are removed in a controlled manner, a couple at a time. Marking may help a beginner sew a more accurate appliqué shape. Eliminate the marking stage as you become more experienced.

4. **Needle-turn the edges of the foreground shapes.** Thread the needle with an 18″ length of thread that closely matches the leaf fabric. Knot the end of the thread.

Clip the basting stitch right at the start of the edge to be turned. Hide the knot underneath the shape and bring the needle up at the point where the thread was clipped, just inside the marked line.

Unpick a couple of stitches along the edge to be turned. Use the point of the needle to sweep under the seam allowance and to adjust the edge of the shape to the marked line (see page 13).

Sew the edge of each leaf with small, concealed stitches (see page 13). Do not remove the basting stitches along the seams that need to remain open.

You need to baste and needle-turn each numbered shape in sequence, as it is very difficult to sew the underneath shapes if they have already been covered by other fabrics.

Repeat Steps 1–4, using the square of petal fabric for the #2 shapes next. When two shapes are side by side, the marked line shared by the shapes may already be basted. Don't remove these stitches; they keep the underlying seam allowance flat and they are a useful guide for needle-turning the overlapping shape. Simply sew over the top of them.

Don't forget that you always baste all the way around each marked shape to secure the fabric firmly onto the background.

Follow Steps 1–4 to attach the center circle. Carefully press the sample on the wrong side to settle the stitches and to sharpen the edges of the appliqué shapes. On the wrong side, all the pattern shapes are clearly defined with stitches. You may cut away the background fabric from behind these shapes to leave just one layer of fabric, apart from seam allowances.

As a rule, I do not cut the back away from quilted items that are going to be well used and well laundered. The intact square of background fabric lends extra stability.

Symmetrical Motif
in a Nutshell

Transfer the pattern onto the WS of the background fabric.

1. Place the appliqué fabric on the RS of the background fabric, working in sequence.

2. On the WS, baste directly on the line, all around the shape, to secure the fabric.

3. On the RS, trim away the excess fabric, leaving a ³⁄₁₆″ seam allowance. Mark the edge to be turned (optional).

4. On the RS, remove the basting stitches, one by one, and needle-turn the seam.

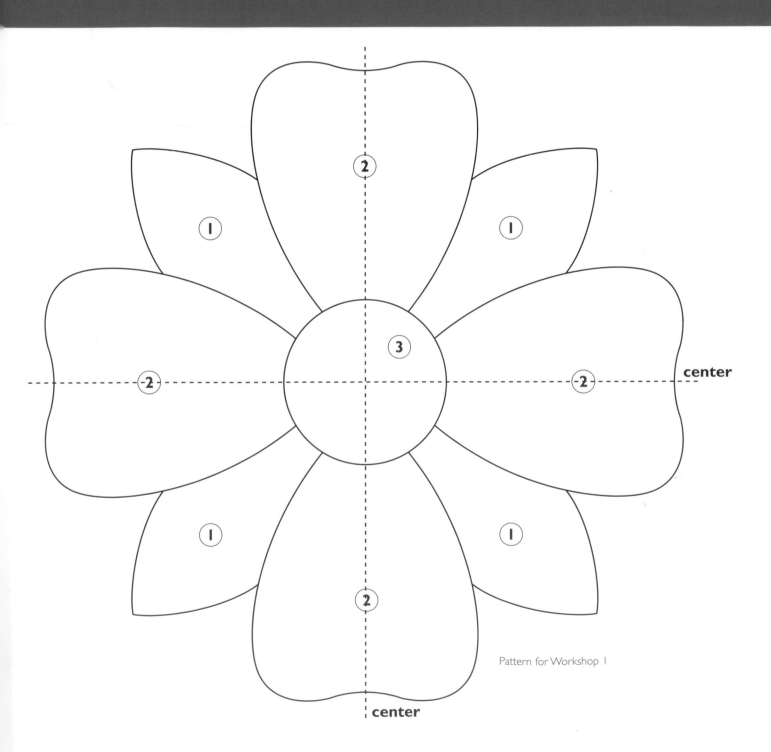

Pattern for Workshop 1

center

center

The Workshop Sample in Use

The workshop sample is machine quilted with lines that echo the shapes. A decorative row of machine stitches and a bright binding complete the sample as a small mat or wallhanging.

Practice the Workshop Skills

You can practice the skills learned in this workshop in Project 1: Dahlia Mat.

Small table mat

project 1 DAHLIA MAT

FINISHED SIZE: 14″

This eye-catching table center is made up of symmetrical shapes with simple lines. Small pieces of hand-dyed fabric used in sequence, from light to dark, give the impression of a luscious dahlia against a painterly background. To finish off the project, the colors are echoed in the fabric, which was chosen to make a continuous line of prairie points around the outer edge.

Fabric Requirements

BACKGROUND FABRIC ½ yard for background circle and backing

FOREGROUND FABRICS ⅛ yard each of green for leaves; dark red, medium red, and rich orange for petals; and light gold for center; ¼ yard medium gold for petals

COMPLEMENTARY FABRIC ½ yard for prairie points and bias binding

BATTING 16″ × 16″

Cutting

BACKGROUND FABRIC Cut 1 square 15″ × 15″ for the front and 1 square 16″ × 16″ for the backing.

FOREGROUND FABRICS

Green: Cut 12 squares 2″ × 2″ for shapes 1 and 5.

Dark red: Cut 8 squares 2¾″ × 2¾″ for shape 2.

Medium red: Cut 4 squares 2¾″ × 2¾″ for shape 3.

Rich orange: Cut 4 squares 2¾″ × 2¾″ for shape 4.

Medium gold: Cut 1 square 5½″ × 5½″ for shape 6.

Light gold: Cut 1 square 4″ × 4″ for shape 7.

COMPLEMENTARY FABRIC Cut 2 strips 4″ wide from selvage to selvage (42″–44″ wide; fabrics may vary) for the prairie points. Remove the selvages and join the strips to make one long strip. Cut and join together sufficient 2″-wide bias strips to measure 52″ for a double binding.

Assembly

1. Prepare a master pattern (see page 20) using the pattern on page 35. Transfer it, centered, onto the wrong side of the 15″ square of background fabric. Don't forget to mark the outer edge.

2. Familiarize yourself with the numerical sequence marked on the pattern. Working with one fabric square at a time and matching the straight grains of the fabric, follow Steps 1–4 from Workshop 1 (pages 29–30) until the design is complete. Press gently.

3. From the wrong side, baste around the marked outer circle to show its position on the right side of the background fabric.

4. Position the prepared top onto the batting and backing fabric, and baste in preparation for hand or machine quilting.

In the machine-sewn sample, the center was closely quilted with rows of small petals. Each appliquéd petal was quilted $1/4''$ inside the edge to echo the shape, and the background was quilted with 3 marked lines of concentric circles, $1/2''$ apart.

5. Prepare a continuous length of at least 41 prairie points, each made from 2″ squares (see page 23). Before cutting away any of the excess fabric, make sure the points fit around the basting stitches that mark the outer edge. Pin the points around the circle, with the raw edges against the basted

line. Sew in place, by hand or machine, with a matching thread and $1/8''$ seam, overlapping the first and last points.

The $1/4''$ seam of the binding strip will cover the $1/8''$ seam used to attach the prairie points.

6. Trim the excess fabric up to the edge of the prairie points. Bind to complete, using the prepared bias binding (see page 21).

Dahlia Table Center, *20″ × 20″, machine template-free appliqué with a fusible web. Connie Evans, Upton, Cheshire, England, 2004*

Dahlia Table Runner, 14″ × 36″, hand appliqué, hand echo quilting. Jenny Thomas, Bomere Heath, Shropshire, England, 2004

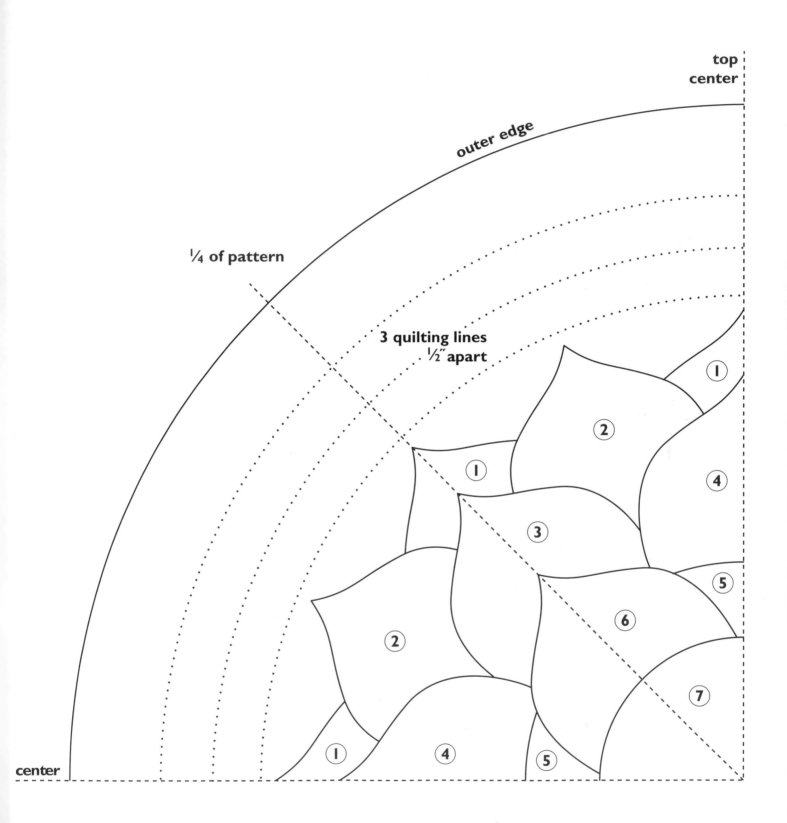

top
center

outer edge

¼ of pattern

3 quilting lines
½" apart

① 2 ④ ⑤

① ③ ⑥ ⑦

2 ① 4 ⑤

center

Template-Free Method by Hand

Asymmetrical Motif on a Dark Background

The skills learned in Workshop 1 are further developed in this workshop to include using dressmaker's carbon paper to transfer a simple pattern onto a dark background. The pattern shapes are reversed on the right side.

FABRIC REQUIREMENTS

BACKGROUND
9″ × 9″ dark fabric

FOREGROUND
2 squares 3″ × 3″ for leaves, 5 squares 3¾″ × 3½″ for petals, and 1 square 2¼″ × 2¼″ for center

OTHER SUPPLIES

THREADS that closely match the foreground fabrics

DRESSMAKER'S CARBON OR TRANSFER PAPER

BALLPOINT PEN

BASIC SEWING SUPPLIES (see page 12)

PREPARATION

Transfer the pattern onto a dark background with dressmaker's carbon paper. Fold the background square to find the centerlines. Secure the square in place with masking tape, wrong side up, on a flat surface. Center the master pattern on top of the square, and hold it in place with pins along the top edge only, outside the marked pattern.

Test the carbon paper to make sure that it transfers, and then carefully slide it underneath the pattern, with the colored side down against the background fabric.

Pin to secure, and then use a ballpoint pen to systematically transfer the pattern lines and number sequence onto the fabric. Before removing the pattern and carbon paper from the fabric, check to see that all the pattern lines have been transferred.

When the pattern is transferred onto the wrong side of the background fabric, the appliqué shapes are reversed on the right side. If you find it difficult to "see" the pattern in reverse, try one of the following adjustments: (1) Trace the master pattern, and then turn the tracing paper over so the reversed pattern is transferred onto the wrong side. (2) If you have a light box, reverse the pattern and trace it onto the wrong side with a marker suitable for dark fabric.

ASSEMBLY

Follow Steps 1–4 from Workshop 1 (page 29).

The Workshop Sample in use

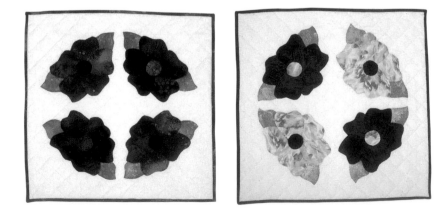

A Pair of Pillows, 16″ × 16″, Loretta Bailey, Bretton, Cheshire, England, 2003. Loretta created a master pattern with the repeated design. She hand quilted a 1″ grid on point on the background, and quilted the appliqué in-the-ditch.

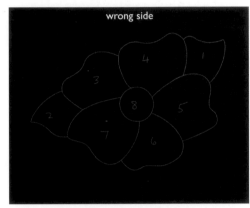

Transfer the pattern onto the wrong side using dressmaker's carbon paper and a ballpoint pen.

wrong side

Pattern transferred onto wrong side

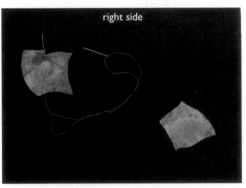

right side

Baste and needle-turn the leaves first.

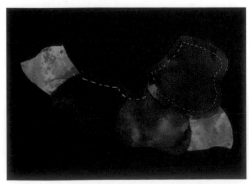

Baste and needle-turn the petals in sequence.

Assymmetrical Motif on a Dark Background
in a Nutshell

Transfer the pattern onto the WS of the background fabric.

1. Place the appliqué fabric on the RS of the background fabric, working in sequence.

2. On the WS, baste directly on the line, all round the shape, to secure the fabric.

3. On the RS, trim away the excess fabric, leaving a ⅛" seam allowance. Mark the edge to be turned (optional).

4. On the RS, remove the basting stitches, one by one, and needle-turn the seam.

Practice the Workshop Skills

You can practice the skills learned in this workshop in Project 2: Jacobean Table Center (page 39) and Project 3: Jacobean Bell Pull (page 41).

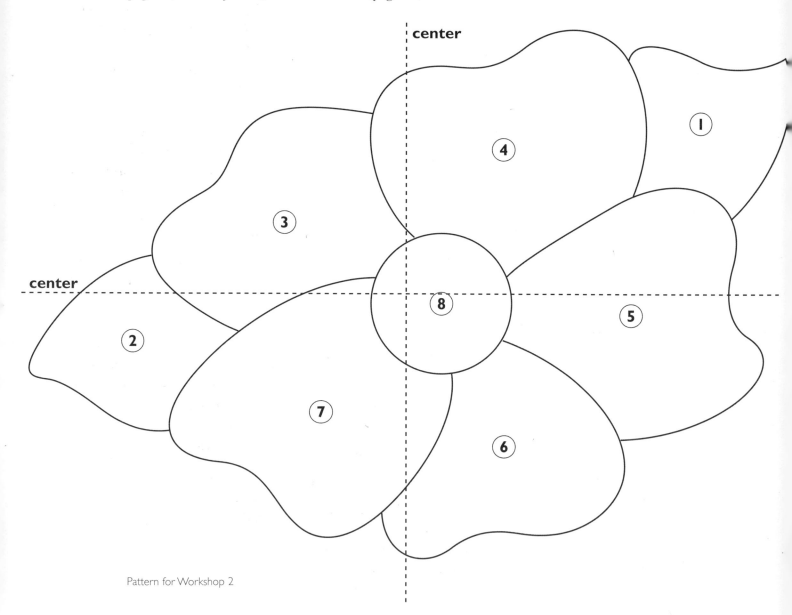

Pattern for Workshop 2

project 2 JACOBEAN TABLE CENTER FINISHED SIZE: 36½"

The four pretty motifs on this table center are Jacobean in style. The shapes are more complex and challenging than those in Project 1 and Workshops 1 and 2, offering you the opportunity to develop your skills. The motifs are embellished with simple stem-stitch embroidery, which adds grace and movement to the design. You will learn how to add borders that are mitered at the corners, which creates space for further embellishment. Individually, each bordered square will make a lovely pillow, but when joined together, they make a striking wall quilt or table center.

Patterns for this project can be found on the pullout and include the four Jacobean motifs. The broken lines on the patterns represent lines to be embroidered.

Remember, these asymmetrical motifs will appear in reverse on the right side of the background fabric.

Fabric Requirements

BACKGROUND FABRIC 2 yards for center square, mitered borders, and binding

FOREGROUND FABRIC ⅛ yard each of pale green and dark green for centers, stems, and leaves; pale peach, medium orange, medium dark terracotta, dark terracotta for flowers and buds

EMBROIDERY THREADS pale green, dark green, medium orange, and dark terracotta

BATTING 38″ × 38″

BACKING 38″ × 38″

Cutting

BACKGROUND FABRIC Cut 4 squares 12½″ × 12½″ and 16 strips 19½″ × 3½″. From the remaining background fabric, cut and join sufficient 2″-wide straight strips to measure 156″ for a double binding.

FOREGROUND FABRIC Because of the complexity of the pattern, the sizes of the rectangles needed for each individual applique shape are not given here. Overlay each pattern shape with a square ruler to estimate the size needed (see page 24).

Assembly

1. For each center square, prepare the master pattern (see page 20), and transfer it, centered, onto the wrong side of the 12½″ square of background fabric.

Do not transfer the embroidery lines. These look more natural when drawn freehand on the right side, after the appliqué is complete.

2. Familiarize yourself with the numerical sequence marked on the pattern. Working with one fabric at a time, follow Steps 1–4 from Workshops 1 and 2 (pages 29 and 36) until the design is complete.

Press gently and trim away the background fabric behind the shapes if preferred.

The pattern shapes in this project are more intricate, so remember to keep the basting stitches small to give a good definition of each shape.

3. On the front of the completed square, use a suitable marker to draw the extra pattern lines for embroidery: the stems joining the leaves, the scrolls, the decorative motifs, and the grid patterns. Use a stem stitch and 2 strands of embroidery thread to define the lines (see next page).

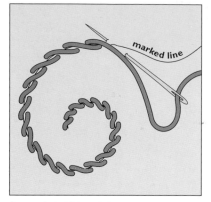

Stem stitch: Make stitches smaller on tighter curves.

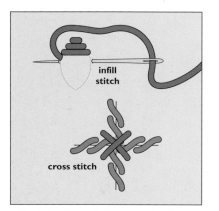

Infill stitch: Cross-stitch over joining lines.

4. Add the $3\frac{1}{2}'' \times 19\frac{1}{2}''$ border strips to the sides of the squares, and miter the corners (see page 29).

5. In preparation for embroidery, transfer the oak leaf and acorn motif that is on pullout accurately and clearly onto the right side of the border fabric. Use the positioning lines on the pattern to center it on the seam of the mitered corner. Define the motifs with a stem stitch, making the stitches smaller on a tight curve, as shown above.

The sample shows the motif on two opposite corners of each square, but this motif can be used on all corners. Another idea is to interpret it as an appliqué design.

6. Repeat Steps 1–5, above, for the remaining 3 squares, and join them together to complete the top of the quilt. Press gently from the wrong side.

7. Mark any hand-quilting lines on the background fabric, using a suitable marker and a ruler (see page 24). Secure the fabric onto the batting and the backing in preparation for hand or machine quilting. Quilt from the center to the edges, quilting as close as possible to each sewn edge to allow the individual shapes to puff up slightly.

The center square of the hand-sewn sample was quilted with diagonal lines at 2″ intervals, and the mitered border was quilted at 1″ intervals.

8. Trim away the excess batting and backing, and bind to complete (see page 26).

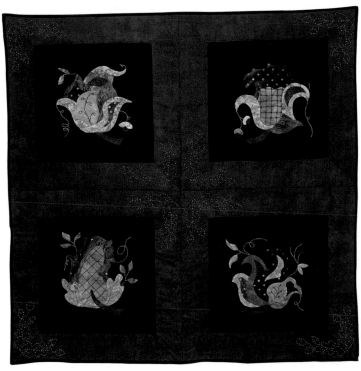

Jacobean Wallhanging, 36″ × 36″, Dot Aellen, Heald Green, Cheshire, England, 2003. Hand appliqué and hand quilting.

A Set of Jacobean Pillows, 18″ × 18″, Jane Hadfield, Cheadle Hulme, Cheshire, England, 2003. Hand appliquéd and hand quilting

At Play With Appliqué

project 3 JACOBEAN BELL PULL FINISHED SIZE: 8″ × 42″

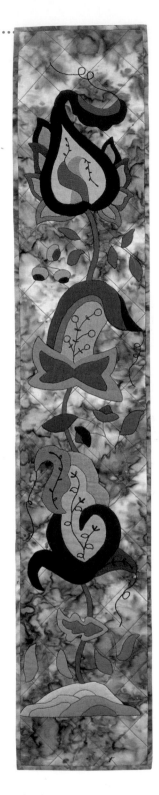

Continuing with the Jacobean theme, this narrow wallhanging offers you the chance to practice and develop your skills using smaller, more intricate shapes. You can make the bell pull to match the table center from Project 2, or you can make one in shaded fabrics, as shown in the project sample. Small pieces of dyed fabrics in three different color families are used for the appliqué shapes to portray the decorative antique bell pulls sewn with shaded crewel wools.

The two halves of the pattern for this project are included on the pullout. The broken lines represent lines to be embroidered.

Fabric Requirements

BACKGROUND FABRIC ½ yard of light to medium colorful fabric for background and binding

FOREGROUND FABRICS The project sample shows three families of color—blue, teal, and pink; within each family, there are six shades—very dark, dark, medium dark, medium, medium light, and light. The position of each color and shade is marked on the pattern.

You will require the following amounts of each shade:

Blue: very dark: 3″ × 3″; dark: 6″ × 6″; medium dark: 7″ × 5″; medium: 7″ × 7″; medium light: 7″ × 7″; light: 9″ × 9″

Teal: very dark: 12″ × 12″; dark: 9″ × 9″; medium dark: 6″ × 6″; medium: 5″ × 5″; medium light: 3″ × 2″; light: 7″ × 7″

Cerise: very dark: 9″ × 13″; dark: 11″ × 12″; medium dark: 12″ × 12″; medium: 9″ × 9″; medium light: 9″ × 9″; light: 9″ × 8″

Teal: very dark: a 22″ strip bias cut at 1¾″ to make ⅝″ wide stems

EMBROIDERY THREADS dark teal, dark blue, and dark cerise

BATTING 12″ × 46″

BACKING 12″ × 46″

Cutting

Background fabric: Cut 1 strip 9″ wide from selvage to selvage (42 - 44″ wide, fabrics may vary). From the remaining background fabric, cut and join sufficient 2″-wide straight strips to measure 112″ for a double binding.

Foreground fabric: Because of the complexity of the pattern, the sizes of the rectangles needed for each individual applique shape are not given here Overlay each pattern shape with a square ruler to estimate the size needed (see page 24).

Assembly

1. Prepare a master pattern (see page 20) using pattern on pullout A. Transfer it, centered, onto the wrong side of the strip of background fabric. Don't forget to mark the outer edge.

If your background fabric is dense, transfer the pattern using a transfer or carbon paper.

2. The stem lines, which go up the center of the wallhanging from flower to flower, must be sewn first. Use a small basting stitch to sew along the marked lines from the back to show the position of the stems on the unmarked front. Start to baste at the beginning of the marked line, and stop at the end.

3. Prepare a fine bias binding tube (³/₁₆″) using a hand-basting method (see page 21). Position the bias tube onto the right side so it is centered over the basting stitches. Overlap the start and end of the line by ½″, and sew in place by hand. Trim the ends of the stem to ¼″.

4. Familiarize yourself with the numerical sequence marked on the pattern. Working with one fabric at a time, follow Steps 1–4 from Workshops 1 and 2 (pages 29 and 36). Keep the basting stitches small for good definition of each intricate shape.

5. On the completed front, use a suitable marker to draw the extra pattern lines for embroidery: the stems joining the leaves, the tendrils and scrolls, and the decorative detail within the flowers. Use a stem stitch and 2 strands of embroidery thread to define the lines (see page 40). You may want to use an infill stitch for the more intricate shapes.

Jacobean Bell Pull, 8″ × 42″, Dot Aellen, Heald Green, Cheshire, England, 2003. Hand appliqué and hand quilting

Jacobean Wallhanging, 15″ × 42″, Jane Hadfield, Cheadle Hulme, Cheshire, England, 2003. Hand appliqué and machine quilting

Jacobean Bell Pull, 8″ × 42″, Beth Stephenson, Cleckheaton, West Yorkshire, England, 2004. Hand appliqué and hand quilting

6. Mark any quilting lines on the background fabric with a suitable marker and a ruler (see page 24). Secure the prepared front onto the batting and backing fabric for hand or machine quilting.

In the machine-sewn sample, black thread was used to sew closely around each shape for definition, and a 2″ diagonal grid was sewn on the background in teal thread.

7. After quilting, trim away the excess fabric from around the edge for a wallhanging measuring 8″ × 42″. Bind the edges (see page 26), and add a ring on the back for hanging to complete.

Jacobean Pillow, 18″ × 18″, Carole Mitson, Fulwood, Lancashire, England, 2004. Machine template-free appliqué method with freezer paper; hand embroidery over the seams

Jacobean Bell Pull, 8″ × 42″, Ethelwyn Taylor, Lytham St. Annes, Lancashire, 2004. Machine template-free appliqué method with freezer paper

Jacobean Rhythms, 13″ × 34″, designed by the author, made by Margaret Robson, Lower Heswall, Wirral, England, 2004. Machine-sewn Bargello background, hand appliqué, and hand quilting

Jacobean Bell Pull, 8″ × 42″, designed by the author, made by Liz Pedley, Drury, Flintshire, Wales, 1992. Hand appliqué and hand quilting

Template-Free Method by Machine
Freezer Paper

For this workshop, freezer paper has the dual function of sticking the pattern in position and stabilizing the fabrics. Freezer paper is easy to see through, so you can trace the pattern accurately, and is easily removed after sewing. The appliqué shapes are basted by machine, and the excess fabric is cut away close to the sewn line. The edges of the shapes are appliquéd with a satin stitch, and then the freezer paper is removed. The pattern shapes are reversed on the right side.

FABRIC REQUIREMENTS

BACKGROUND
9″ × 9″ light fabric

FOREGROUND
1 green square 8″ × 8″ for leaves (or 5 squares 2½″ × 2½″), 1 peach square 6″ × 6″ for petals, and 1 yellow square 3″ × 3″ for center

OTHER SUPPLIES

MACHINE THREADS that closely match the foreground fabrics

FREEZER PAPER 8½″ × 8½″

PENCIL OR PERMANENT MARKER

SMALL, SHARP SCISSORS

SMALL SAFETY PINS

BASIC SEWING SUPPLIES (see page 12)

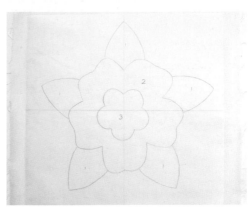

Transfer traced pattern onto wrong side.

A symmetrical pattern looks the same on the right side of the background fabric, but an asymmetrical pattern is reversed.

PREPARATION

Transfer the pattern onto the background with freezer paper. Fold the freezer paper square to find the center. Center the freezer paper, dull side up, on the master pattern and trace all the pattern lines. Using a hot, steam-free iron and a firm ironing board, press to stick the freezer paper so it is centered, dull side up, on the wrong side of the background fabric.

ASSEMBLY

1. Place the shapes on the background fabric. Place the fabric for the leaves, right sides up, on the unmarked side (the right side) of the background fabric. Safety pin the 4 corners to hold the layers together.

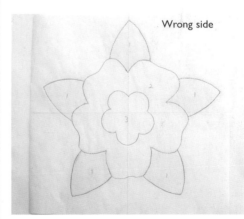

Place fabric on the right side; pin in place.

To make Step 1 easier, all the leaves are cut from one large square. If you find this wasteful for future projects, cut a small rectangle for each separate shape.

2. Machine baste the shapes onto the background fabric. With the marked side of the freezer paper uppermost, sew all around the leaf shapes where the fabric will be appliquéd. Sew directly on the line, using a thread that matches the fabric and a small, tight stitch. If you are competent with free-motion sewing, use that method to attach the shapes.

Sew around the leaf shapes on marked paper pattern.

A thread that matches the fabric is an ideal choice, but this means changing the thread for each color change in the fabric. You may opt to use a neutral thread, such as beige, gray, or lilac, with a light neutral on light to medium fabrics and a dark neutral on medium to dark fabrics. Consider using an invisible thread on the bobbin when machine basting a variety of colors.

3. Trim the foreground shapes. On the right side, the leaf shapes are defined by stitches. Remove the safety pins, and trim the excess fabric by cutting as close as possible to the outside of the stitches

Keep your scissors flat so you can get close to the stitches.

Trim excess fabric close to the stitched line on right side.

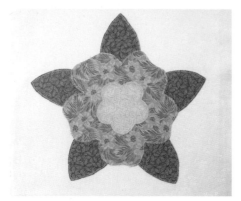

Appliqué petals and center motif.

Satin stitch around edges; work from background to foreground.

Sew with contrasting thread for greater definition of shapes.

Repeats Steps 1–3 above to appliqué the fabric for the petals. Separate the petals by basting along the dotted lines of the pattern, or simply define the outer and inner edges.

Repeat Steps 1–3 for the center motif to complete. Do not remove the freezer paper yet.

4. Machine appliqué the foreground shapes. Set up your machine for a satin stitch (see page 18) and use threads to match the fabrics. To give the impression that they are lying underneath, you must first sew the shapes that are overlapped.

Following the numbered sequence, work from the right side of the background fabric where the foreground shapes are visible. Satin stitch around the edges of each leaf shape first.

When defining the petals, try to sew smooth curves, sewing along the dotted line of the pattern to give an overlapped appearance. Sew around the center motif to complete the machine appliqué.

The satin stitch perforates the freezer paper, making it easy to remove without disturbing the stitches. Peel the freezer paper away from behind the pattern shapes and around the edges.

• •

A small sliver of freezer paper will be trapped behind the satin stitch. This is not a problem, unless the pattern lines are marked with an unsuitable marker that could bleed into the fabrics.

The Workshop Sample in Use

Floral Pillow, 18″ x 18″, Kath Lloyd, Drury, Flintshire, Wales, 2003. Kath repeated the workshop pattern and joined the blocks together with narrow strips to create a pillow with an overlapped back

Machine Template-Free Method
with Freezer Paper *in a Nutshell*

Transfer the pattern by ironing the freezer paper onto the WS of the background fabric.

1. Place and pin the appliqué fabric on the RS, working in sequence.

2. On the WS, machine baste directly on the line, all around the shape, to secure the fabric.

3. On the RS, trim away the excess fabric, right up to the stitches.

4. On the RS, satin stitch the cut edges in sequence, and remove the freezer paper from the WS.

Practice the Workshop Skills

You can practice the skills learned in this workshop in Project 4: Pansy Bell Pull.

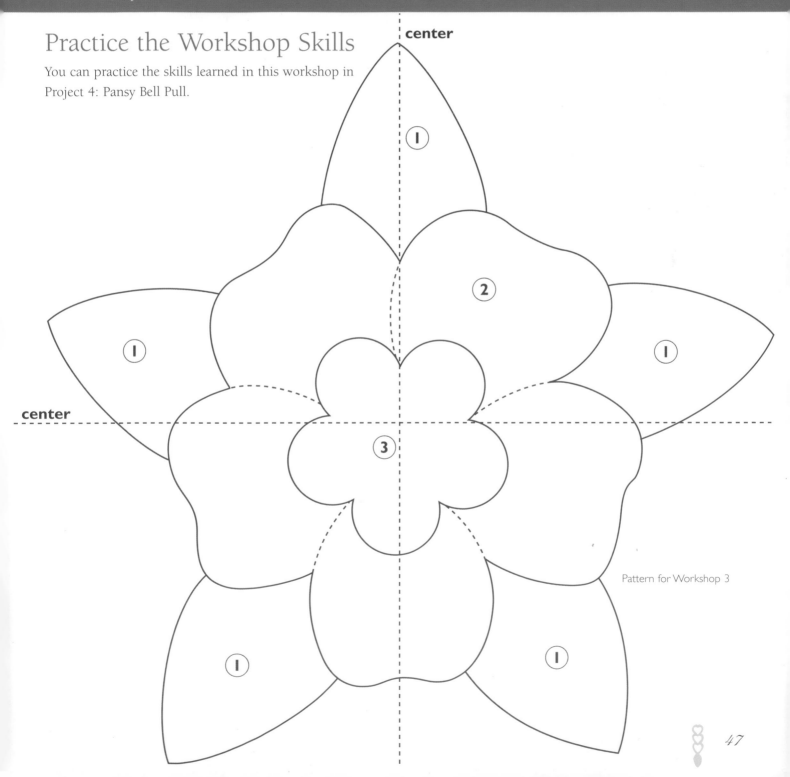

center

center

Pattern for Workshop 3

project 4 PANSY BELL PULL

FINISHED SIZE: 9″ × 42″

As a teacher, I soon became aware of the popularity of these bell pull wallhangings with my students. These projects are quickly made, compact to handle, and easy to display in most homes. Here is another floral bell pull for you to practice the machine appliqué method using freezer paper.

For simplicity, each flower head is made from one self-colored textured fabric, and the individual petals are defined with the zigzag stitch. The stems are also simply defined with a zigzag stitch.

To develop the idea, try using a different fabric for each petal and applique a narrow strip for the stems. See the gallery on page 49 to enjoy the endless possibilities of this simple idea for a floral wallhanging.

The two halves of the pattern for this project are included on the pullout.

Fabric Requirements

BACKGROUND FABRIC ⅝ yard light fabric for front and binding

FOREGROUND FABRICS ¼ yard dark green for leaves

1 square 10″ × 10″ each of orange, plum, purple, and red for pansies

1 square 2″ × 2″ each of mauve and yellow for centers

2 squares 2″ × 2″ of black for centers

MACHINE THREADS choose threads to match the foreground fabrics: flowers, leaves, and centers

BATTING 13″ × 46″

BACKING 13″ × 46″

FREEZER PAPER 9″ × 33″

Cutting

BACKGROUND FABRIC Cut 1 strip 10″ wide from selvage to selvage (42″–44″, fabrics may vary). From the remaining background fabric, cut and join sufficient 2″-wide straight strips to measure 106″ for a double binding.

Assembly

1. Prepare a master pattern (see page 20). Find and mark the centerlines on the paper side of the freezer paper, and trace the pattern onto it. Iron the freezer paper onto the center of the wrong side of the 10″ strip of background fabric.

2. Familiarize yourself with the numerical sequence marked on the pattern. Define the stems with a straight stitch on the paper side first and zigzag along these lines on the right side. Working with one fabric square at a time, follow Steps 1–4 from Workshop 3 (page 44) until the appliqué is complete. If you are using 1 fabric for each flower, make sure the lines separating the petals are defined at the basting stage so they can be redefined at the stitching stage.

3. Peel away the perforated freezer paper, and press the strip from the reverse.

4. On the completed front, mark any quilting lines on the background, leaves, and flowers. Secure the prepared front onto the batting and backing fabric for hand or machine quilting.

The machine-sewn sample was quilted with a 1½″ diagonal grid marked at 45° (see page 24).

5. After quilting, trim away the excess fabric from around the edge for a wallhanging measuring 9″ × 42″. Use a large ruler and rotary cutter to shape the top and the bottom to 45°. Bind the edges (see page 26), and add a ring on the back for hanging to complete.

The same motifs were used to make the wallhanging shown here, using the hand method described in Workshop 2 (page 36). The stems were defined with bias tubes, and the petals were made from individual fabrics. Hand quilting gives the wallhanging a softer texture, and prairie points add extra interest and color to the top edge. The tubes for the hanging tabs were made from 5″ × 2″ fabric strips, sewn into the binding on the back (see page 26). The single binding strip was prepared from joined 1¼″ × 2″ lengths of pansy fabrics.

Pansy and Prairie Points, 18″ × 18″

INSPIRATIONAL FLORAL WALLHANGINGS AND PILLOWS

Daffodils, 10″ × 42″, Dilys Fronks, 1998. Machine template-free appliqué with freezer paper and machine quilting

Anemonies, 10″ × 42″, Liz Pedley, Drury, Flintshire, Wales, 2002. Machine template-free appliqué with batting and foundation fabric, and hand quilting

Anemonies, 10″ × 42″, Dilys Fronks, 2000. Hand appliqué and machine quilting

Irises, 10″ × 41″, Loretta Bailey, Bretton, Cheshire, England, 2001. Hand appliqué and hand echo quilting

Irises, 12″ × 36″, Kath Lloyd,
Drury, Flintshire, Wales, 2001.
Hand appliqué on a patchwork
background and machine quilting

Irises, 10″ × 41″, Dilys Fronks, 2000.
Hand appliqué and machine quilting

Roses, 10″ × 42″, Dilys Fronks, 1996.
Hand appliqué and hand quilting

Poppies, 10″ × 42″, Dilys Fronks, 1996.
Hand appliqué and hand quilting

Poppy Pillow, 18″ × 18″, Dilys Fronks, 1996.
Hand appliqué and hand quilting

Rose Pillow, 18″ × 18″, Dilys Fronks, 1996.
Hand appliqué and hand quilting

Daffodil Pillow, 18″ × 18″, Dilys Fronks, 1997.
Hand appliqué and hand quilting

Template-Free Method by Machine
Batting and a Lightweight Foundation Fabric

This workshop is a development of the freezer paper method from Workshop 3. A lightweight foundation fabric, such as muslin, is easy to see through, so the pattern can be traced accurately. The foundation fabric also acts as a protective cover on the back to prevent the batting from getting into the bobbin case of the machine. Because this fabric is not removed after sewing, it adds an extra layer to the project.

The shapes are quilted at the same time that they are appliquéd with a satin stitch. The pattern shapes are reversed on the right side.

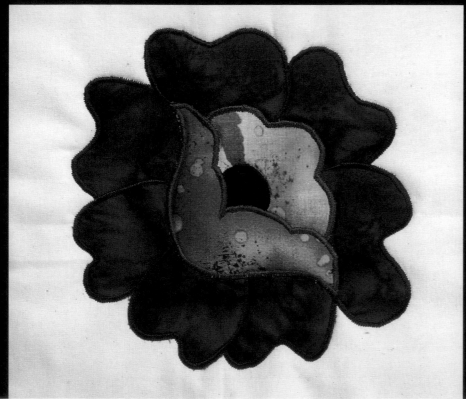

FABRIC REQUIREMENTS

BACKGROUND
9″ × 9″ light fabric

FOREGROUND
1 red square 7″ × 7″ for outer petals (or 1 square 3½″ × 3½″ per petal), 1 orange square 3″ × 3″ for back inner petals, 1 orange square 4″ × 4″ for front inner petals, and 1 black square 1½″ × 1½″ for center motif

LIGHTWEIGHT FOUNDATION FABRIC
9″ × 9″ muslin

BATTING
9″ × 9″

OTHER SUPPLIES

MACHINE THREADS that closely match the foreground fabrics

PENCIL OR PERMANENT MARKER

SMALL, SHARP SCISSORS

SMALL SAFETY PINS

BASIC SEWING SUPPLIES (see page 12)

Trace the pattern; baste layers together.

Place fabric on right side; pin in place.

Baste around shapes from the wrong side to appliqué fabric to right side. Trim excess fabric right up to stitches.

Appliqué remaining shapes; satin stitch edges in sequence.

PREPARATION

Transfer the pattern onto the foundation by tracing. Trace the master pattern onto the center of the foundation fabric using a suitable marker.

A permanent marker gives a heavy line that can be seen on both sides of the foundation fabric. You can reverse the foundation fabric so the appliqué shapes will not be reversed on the right side.

Prepare the batting sandwich by placing the background fabric right side down on a flat surface. Cover it with the batting, and place the foundation fabric on top, marked side up. Check that the raw edges are level, and baste the layers together around the outer edge.

ASSEMBLY

Follow Steps 1–4 as detailed in Workshop 3 (page 44).

The satin stitch is sewn through the three layers of the batting sandwich. Practice to find out if your machine sews the layers better with a quilting foot.

The foundation fabric is the back of the piece of work, and it can remain for a project, such as a pillow front, where it cannot be seen. For a project with a visible back, you can cover this layer with a backing fabric at the basting stage, so the satin stitch is seen on the back, or at the quilting stage when the stitches will hold all the layers together.

The Workshop Sample in Use

Liz's Handkerchief Quilt, 60″ x 84″, designed by the author, made by Liz Pedley, Drury, Flintshire, Wales, 1998. The inspiration came from embroidered motifs on old handkerchiefs. The flower for Workshop 4 was taken from this quilt and simplified.

Batting and lightweight foundation fabric
in a Nutshell

Transfer the pattern onto the foundation by tracing and prepare the batting sandwich.

1. Place and pin the applique fabrics on the RS, working in sequence.

2. On the WS, machine baste directly on the line, all around the shape, to secure the fabric.

3. On the RS, trim away the excess fabric, right up to the stitches,

4. On the RS, satin stitch the cut edges in sequence.

Practice the Workshop Skills

You can practice the skills learned in this workshop in Project 5: Tulip Table Center (page 52).

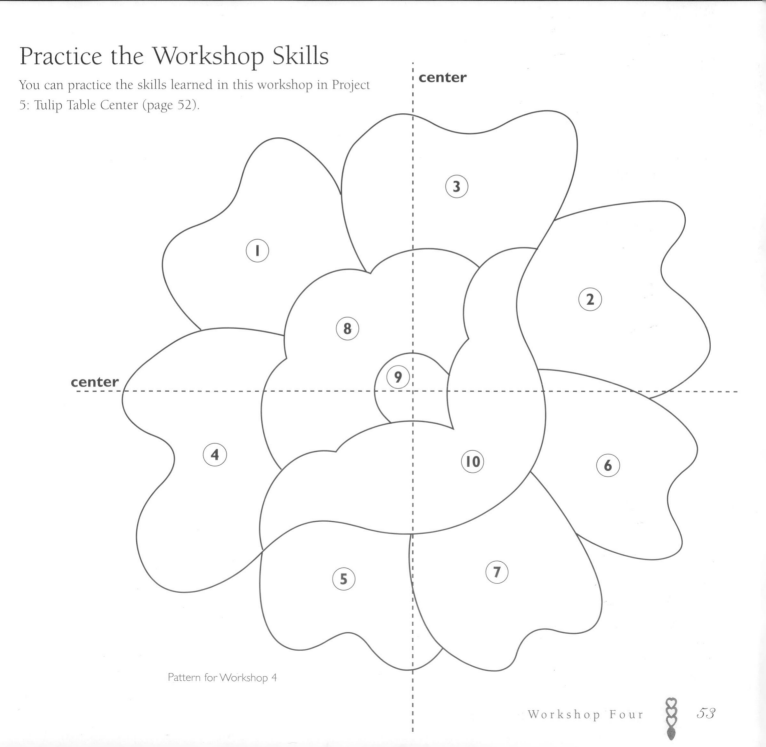

Pattern for Workshop 4

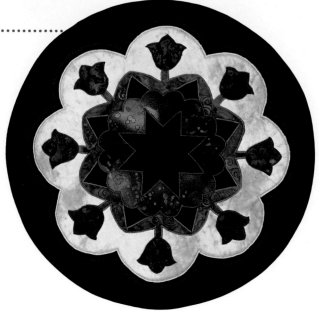

project 5 TULIP TABLE CENTER

FINISHED SIZE: 18″ CIRCLE

I have always been fond of hearts and circular motifs, and so this dramatic table center is a particular favorite. The hearts form a ring around the center, overlapping slightly to define a central star. Each heart supports a stylized tulip, with leaves that touch to form the points of another star. To contrast with the star, a softly curved border is added and echoed with bright decorative machine stitches. Make this attractive project in colors to match your decor for an eye-catching display. For a large table, increase the size of the pattern on a photocopier.

Fabric Requirements

The background fabric is black in this sample. Choose opaque foreground fabrics to make sure the background doesn't show through the other layers.

FOUNDATION FABRIC: 19″ × 19″ lightweight fabric, such as muslin

BACKGROUND FABRIC: 19″ × 19″ black fabric

FOREGROUND FABRICS: 1 square 16″ × 16″ yellow

1 square 10¾″ × 10¾″ green for leaves

8 squares 2¾″ × 2¾″ red for tulips

1 square 8½″ × 8½″ cerise for ring of hearts

MACHINE THREADS: choose threads to match the fabrics

BATTING: 19″ × 19″

BACKING: 19″ × 19″

BINDING: 11″ × 11″ black fabric; cut and join sufficient 1¼″-wide bias strips to measure 68″ for a single binding

Assembly

1. Prepare a master pattern (see page 20), and trace it onto the foundation fabric. Prepare the batting sandwich as outlined in Workshop 4 (page 44), using the black square, batting, and the foundation square.

This is a larger project than the workshop sample, so use more safety pins to keep the fabrics flat and the edges level.

2. Familiarize yourself with the numerical sequence marked on the pattern. Working with one fabric at a time, follow the steps 1–3 in Workshop 3 and 4 (page 36). Add the backing layer after all the appliqué shapes have been basted, and pin well.

Follow Step 4 from Workshops 3 and 4 to stitch the raw edges with a machine satin stitch through all the layers.

You need to add an extra layer to the back of this project to cover the marked muslin layer. For a pillow project, the pillow back covers the muslin.

3. Mark and quilt the lines radiating from the center to define the points of the star. Add a line of decorative machine stitching about ½″ from the curved outer edge of the pattern, using the width of the machine foot as a guide.

4. Trim the outer edge to make an 18″ circle, and bind to complete (see page 26).

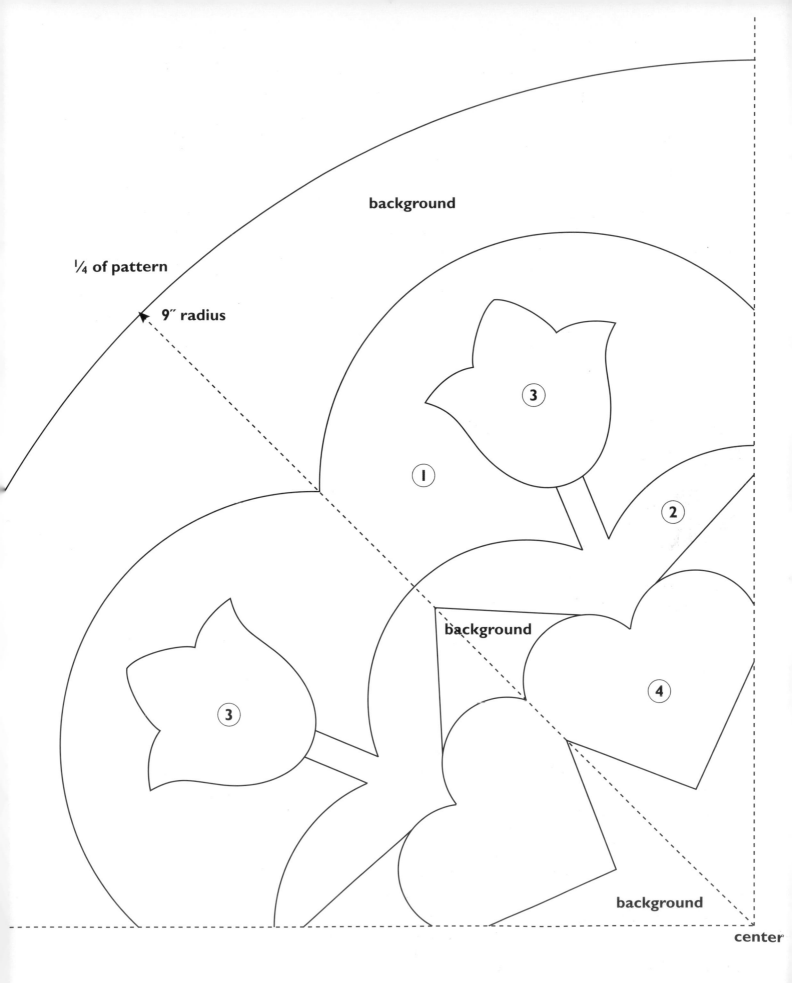

background

¼ of pattern

9″ radius

background

background

center

Tulip Table Center Pattern

Christmas Tulip Pillow, 18″ × 18″, Dilys Fronks, 2004. Hand appliqué and machine quilting

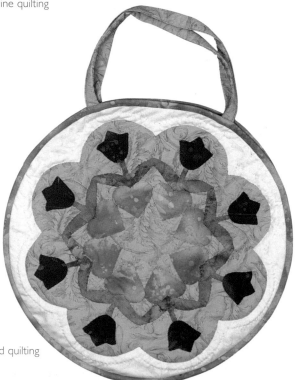

Tulip Bag, 18″, Jenny Thomas, Bomere Heath,
Shropshire, England, 2004. Hand appliqué and hand quilting

Template-Free Method by Hand or Machine
Bias Binding

In this workshop, the fabric shapes are appliquéd onto a background "sky" fabric that forms part of the finished project. The shapes are basted onto a lightweight foundation fabric that stays in place when the sewing is complete. The excess fabric is cut away close to the sewn line and the edges are covered with prepared bias strips instead of satin stitches. The pattern shapes are reversed on the right side. The outer line of the pattern is part of the overall design and is defined with a straight-cut binding strip, which is sewn on after the sample is quilted.

FABRIC REQUIREMENTS

BIAS TUBES
10″ × 10″ print fabric

BACKGROUND
9″ × 9″ sky fabric

FOREGROUND
1 purple square 2″ × 2″ for center, 1 maroon square 5½″ × 5½″ for petals, 1 square 7¾″ × 7¾″ for leaves (Choose these to complement the bias binding fabric.)

BINDING
⅛ yard

Cut and join sufficient 2″-wide straight strips of the same print fabric to measure 46″ for a double binding.

BATTING
12″ × 12″

BACKING FABRIC
12″ × 12″

OTHER SUPPLIES

PENCIL OR SUITABLE MARKER

MASKING TAPE

BASTING THREAD that contrasts with appliqué fabrics

¼″ BIAS BAR for preparation of bias bars by machine

SEWING THREAD that closely matches bias binding

BOARD, CUTTER, AND RULER

BASIC SEWING SUPPLIES (see page 12)

Floral Hanging 16″ × 32″, Loretta Bailey, Bretton, Cheshire, England, 1999. Hand bias method and hand quilting

Poppies and Pansies in the Window, 16″ × 48″, Dilys Fronks, 1999. Hand bias method and machine quilting

Floral Pillows, 16″ × 16″, Loretta Bailey, Bretton, Cheshire, England, 1999. Hand bias method and hand quilting

Grow to the Light, 24″ × 36″, Dilys Fronks, 2003. Machine bias method and machine quilting

Clematis Window, 16″ × 21″, Dilys Fronks, 2000. Machine bias method with iron-on bias binding and machine quilted

Hollyhocks Window, 16″ × 32″, Dilys Fronks, 2000. Machine bias method with iron-on bias binding and machine quilting

project 7 TIGER LILIES WALLHANGING

FINISHED SIZE: 26″ × 43¾″

My favorite expression, "I feel a quilt coming on," was foremost in my mind when visiting an aunt several years ago. Knowing of my interest in textiles, she showed me tablecloths that had been made many years ago by her mother. They were lovingly sewn, using a cutwork embroidery technique, with iron-on transfers. As I enjoyed them, my creative juices started to flow, and I mentally started to play with the idea of interpreting cutwork as a quiltmaking technique. The bias appliqué method, outlined in Workshop 5 (page 57), seemed an ideal way of solving this creative puzzle. I have outlined below the creative steps I followed as I developed the pattern inspired by one of the tablecloths. The paterns for this project are included on the pullout.

Tiger Lilies Wallhanging, Dilys Fronks and Loretta Bailey, Bretton, Cheshire

Developing an Idea

STEP 1: The starting point was a photograph of the motif at the center of the cloth. I doodled pattern ideas on a scrap of paper.

Cutwork tablecloth, 48″ × 48″. Owned by Dorothy Morgan, Griffithstown, Monmouthshire, Wales

STEP 2: I drafted the chosen pattern to a comfortable working size.

STEP 3: I appliquéd the infill fabric first to represent the cutout areas. The sample shown here (on the left) was made to resemble the tablecloth, with the shapes defined by machine satin stitches.

Left: infill background and satin stitch. Right: infill background, sheer fabrics, and satin stitch

STEP 4: I repeated the sample with sheer fabrics (on the right) coloring the flowers, leaves, and buds.

STEP 5: I then experimented by viewing the sample as a mirror image.

Mirror image, with infill background, sheer fabrics, and satin stitch

STEP 6: I then had the final pattern.

Any of these developmental patterns shown in the steps can be increased on a photocopier to any size and used for this project. I chose to enlarge the final pattern by 170% to make it suitable for use with a ¼″ bias binding.

Fabric Requirements

BACKGROUND FABRIC 1 yard neutral for front

FOREGROUND FABRICS 1/8 yard yellow

3/8 yard orange

3/8 yard red

1/4 yard neutral for stems

1/2 yard green for leaves

1/3 yard brown tone-on-tone for infill

BIAS BINDING FABRICS 1/4 yard dark yellow

1/4 yard dark orange

1/4 yard dark red

1/4 yard dark brown

1/2 yard dark green

EDGE BINDING FABRIC fat 1/4 yard medium green

BATTING 29″ × 44″

BACKING 29″ × 44″ plus 1 strip 27″ × 4 1/2″ for a hanging sleeve

THREADS choose threads to match the bias fabrics; brown embroidery thread to add detail to the flowers (optional)

Cutting

BACKGROUND FABRIC Cut 1 rectangle 27″ × width of fabric (selvage to selvage).

FOREGROUND FABRICS Cut rectangles as follows:

- **Yellow flower:** Cut 4 strips 6″ × 4″.
- **Orange flower:** Cut 4 strips 9″ × 10″.
- **Red flower:** Cut 4 squares 9″ × 9″.
- **Stems:** Cut 8 strips 2″ × 5″ and 4 strips 4″ × 3″.
- **Leaves:** Cut 2 rectangles 6″ × 20″ for vertical leaves and 1 strip 8″ × 24″ for horizontal leaves.
- **Brown infill:** Cut 1 strip 10″ × 40″.

BIAS BINDING Prepare bias tubes using a hand or machine method (see page 21) at the following lengths:

- **Dark yellow:** 1 3/4 yards
- **Dark orange:** 5 1/2 yards
- **Dark red:** 5 1/2 yards
- **Dark brown:** 2 1/2 yards
- **Dark green:** 10 1/2 yards

BINDING Cut and join sufficient 1 1/4″-wide bias cut strips to measure 4 yards for a single binding.

Assembly

1. Prepare a master pattern (see page 20), and trace it, centered, onto the wrong side of the background fabric. Mark the outer edge, but do not cut it to shape at this stage.

2. Working with one fabric at a time, follow Steps 1–3 from Workshop 5 (page 58) to attach the foreground shapes onto the right side of the background fabric.

3. Study the master pattern to familiarize yourself with the placement and the sewing sequence for the bias tubes. Bind the raw edges of the shapes by following Step 4 from Workshop 5 (page 58). Appliqué the bias tubes, in sequence, using matching threads and small, concealed stitches (see page 13). In the sample, I chose not to add the stamens to the flowers, but if you want to include them, use 2 strands of brown embroidery thread to define them.

4. Press gently from the reverse, and turn to the right side to mark any quilting lines on the background fabric, using a ruler and a suitable marker (see page 24).

The hand-sewn sample was quilted with threads to match the fabrics. Each appliqué shape was echoed by sewing 1/4″ in from the edges of the bias binding. The background fabric was quilted with vertical lines, 2″ apart, and the central shape, enclosed by the leaves, was quilted with a 1″ grid.

5. Secure the background, right sides up, onto the batting and backing, ready for quilting.

6. Trim and shape the outer edges to the pattern line, and bind the raw edges (see page 26). Prepare a single hanging sleeve (see page 25), and attach it by hand just below the shaped edge to complete.

Template-Free Method by Hand
Reverse Appliqué

The pattern, which has the appearance of a stencil, is transferred onto the right side of the foreground fabric. The background fabrics are then positioned behind each shape and sewn using a needle-turn method. There is no reversal of the pattern on the right side

FABRIC REQUIREMENTS

BACKGROUND

$6\frac{1}{2}'' \times 6\frac{1}{2}''$ medium blue for flower and $7\frac{1}{2}'' \times 7\frac{1}{2}''$ cerise for flower center and outer circle

FOREGROUND

$9'' \times 9''$ light blue fabric

OTHER SUPPLIES

THREAD that closely matches the foreground fabric

DRESSMAKER'S CARBON PAPER

BALLPOINT PEN

BASIC SEWING SUPPLIES (see page 12)

PREPARATION

Transfer the pattern onto the foreground fabric. Transfer the master pattern so it is centered on the right side of the foreground fabric. If you are using a light fabric, trace the pattern; for dark fabrics, use dressmaker's carbon paper and the method detailed in Workshop 2 (page 36).

Think of the pattern as a series of holes. Draw around a hole, and put a tick in the center. This tick transfers onto the foreground fabric, and when you start to sew, it is a useful reminder of the shapes that are cut out.

To make it easier to get the point of the scissors into the foreground fabric after you have basted the layers together, snip the center of each shape that is to be cut away.

ASSEMBLY

1. Place the background fabrics behind the foreground shapes. Place the square of flower fabric right side up on a flat surface. Place the foreground fabric on top, also right side up, to show the marked lines. Make sure the background fabric extends beyond the edges of the marked shape to give a "comfort zone." Do this by feel or by holding the square up to the light to see the shadowing of one fabric against the other. Pin the fabrics together to prepare for basting.

In reverse appliqué, because you cut large holes from the foreground fabric, it is very important to match the straight grains of the fabric layers. By basting the fabric layers together before cutting, you maintain stability.

2. Baste the shapes. To hold the fabrics together, hand baste from the right side around each marked shape where the fabric is to be sewn. Using small, regular stitches, baste ¼" outside the marked pattern line. Try to keep the fabrics flat so there is no movement between the layers. Remove the pins.

Transfer the pattern onto the right side using dressmaker's carbon paper and mark the holes.

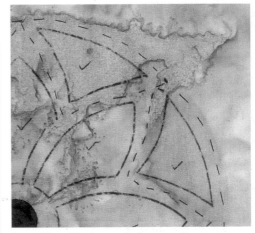
Baste ¼" outside the marked pattern lines.

Needle-turn the edge; remove basting stitches.

Trim the excess fabric to leave a small seam allowance.

Needle-turn the remaining fabric.

Trim the excess fabric to complete.

To allow sufficient space for needle-turning the seam, avoid basting closer than ¼".

3. **Needle-turn the edges.** Working one shape at a time, with the right side uppermost, cut the foreground fabric away inside the marked pattern line, leaving ³⁄₁₆" seam allowance.

Do not be tempted to cut out all the shapes before starting. Doing so encourages instability and distortion in the foreground fabric.

Prepare the seam allowances for needle-turning by clipping where necessary (see page 14). Use a thread that closely matches the foreground fabric to needle-turn and secure the edges to the marked line (see page 14). After sewing the shapes, remove the basting stitches. Carefully press the sample from the back to settle the stitches and sharpen the edges of the shapes.

4. **Trim the background fabric.** On the wrong side, small stitches define the sewn shapes. Trim the excess background fabric outside these stitches, leaving a scant ¼" seam allowance around each shape. Don't forget to trim the fabric from behind the marked center circle. Press lightly.

Follow Steps 1–4 above with the remaining fabric. Press carefully.

The Workshop Sample in use

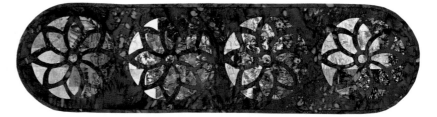

Seasons, 9″ × 36″, Liz Pedley, Drury, Flintshire, Wales, 2004. Liz used the repeated pattern as a window motif to make this small wallhanging. She cut 2″ × 2″ squares of floral fabrics and sewed them together to create scenes suggesting spring, summer, autumn, and winter

Reverse Appliqué *in a Nutshell*

Transfer the pattern onto the RS of the foreground fabric.

1. Place the background fabrics, in sequence, behind the shapes marked on the foreground.

2. On the RS, baste ¼″ outside the line marked on the fore-ground fabric.

3. On the RS, cut on the inside of the marked line to leave a scant ³⁄₁₆″ seam allowance. Needle-turn the edge of the foreground fabric to the background.

4. On the WS, trim the excess background fabric to leave a scant ¼″ seam allowance outside the stitches.

Practice the Workshop Skills

You can practice the skills learned in this workshop in Project 8: Ring Around the Butterflies Tablecloth (page 70).

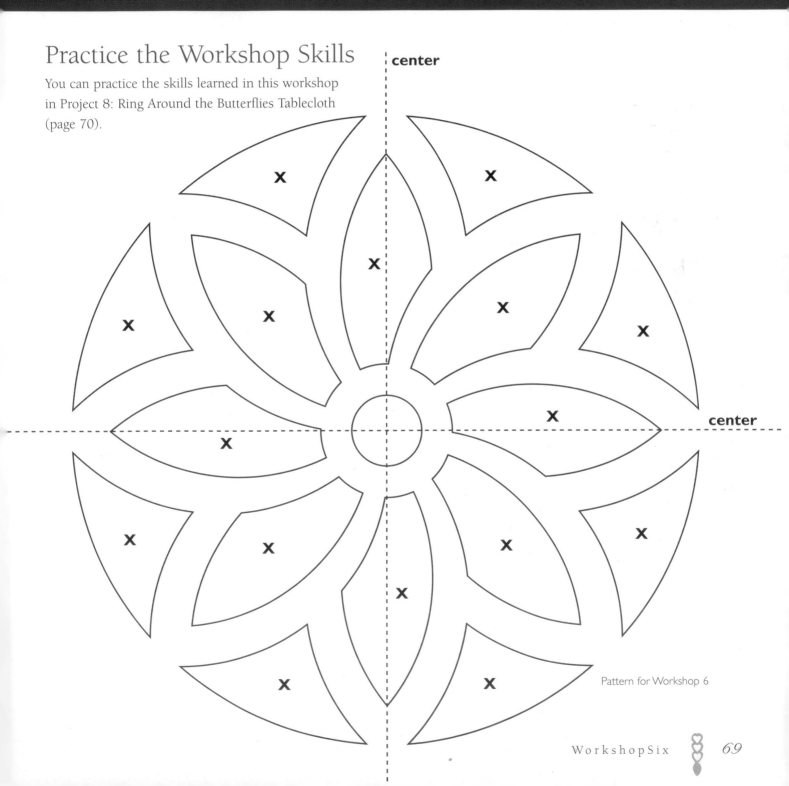

Pattern for Workshop 6

project 8 RING AROUND THE BUTTERFLIES TABLECLOTH

FINISHED SIZE: 24½″ × 24½″

Butterflies are beautiful creatures, filling the countryside with flashes of color and unrestrained delicacy as they flit from flower to flower. They make a wonderful source of inspiration because the wing shapes are simple to draw and can be interpreted in any color imaginable—to match the decor or to interpret the mood of the moment. One pattern square alone, with a border and a ruffle, makes a pretty pillow. However, to practice the skills of Workshop 6 (page 66), this project has four squares sewn together to create a secondary design.

The sample shows the butterflies in the center, enclosed by the flower stems. By rotating the block, the flowers cluster in the center, and the butterflies move to the corners (see *Freda's Butterflies*, page 72). You can choose to make the butterfly wing with a single fabric or you can develop your skills by creating your own fabric for a fragmented wing, using a paper foundation method. The pattern for this project is included on the pullout.

Fabric Requirements

FOREGROUND FABRIC ⅞ yard white tone-on-tone

BACKGROUND FABRICS 4 squares 4½″ × 4½″ yellow floral for flowers

4 squares 2″ × 2″ red for flower centers

8 strips 7″ × 2″ medium green for stems

16 strips 4½″ × 2½″ dark leafy green for each pair of leaves

4 squares 4½″ × 4½″ green for butterfly bodies

4 squares 8½″ × 8½″ medium floral for each pair of simple wings

BATTING 26″ × 26″

BACKING 26″ × 26″

BINDING FABRIC Cut and join sufficient 1¼″-wide bias strips to measure 106″ for a single binding.

OPTIONAL FRAGMENTED WINGS BY MACHINE 8 sheets 4″ × 8″ of tracing paper, 2″ strips floral fabrics in medium and dark, and 2″ strips bright accent color

Cutting

FOREGROUND FABRIC Cut 4 squares 13½″ × 13½″.

Assembly

1. Prepare a master pattern (see page 13) using the pattern on pullout 2,

and transfer it onto the right side of the foreground squares.

2. Follow Steps 1–4 from Workshop 6 (page 66) until the design is complete. If you wish to fragment the wings, prepare the fabric in advance by following the method detailed on the next page.

• • • • • • • • • • • • • • • • •

After you have turned and trimmed the flower fabric, use a stencil to draw a circle on this fabric, and follow the procedure described in step 2 to reveal the red fabric for the centers.

3. Reduce the squares to measure 12½″ × 12½″, and join them together with a ¼″ seam, with either the flowers or the butterflies together in the center. Mark lines in preparation for quilting and place the joined squares, right side up, on the batting and backing.

The sample was hand quilted in-the-ditch on the background fabrics, with an echo line to emphasize each shape. A 2″ diagonal grid was quilted on the foreground fabric to unite the 4 squares.

4. Trim away the excess batting and backing, and gently round off the corners. Bind with the prepared strip to complete (see page 26).

Preparing a Fragmented Wing

1. Trace the wing pattern and numerical sequence onto the tracing paper squares for a machine method. You must sew 1 wing in each pair with the tracing reversed to give a mirror image of the pattern. Sew the straight edges of the strips onto the paper, in sequence, along the marked lines.

Make sure the fabrics extend generously—a good ½″—beyond the outer edges of the marked pattern. They will be trimmed after the wing is sewn in place.

2. Pin the fabric for shape 1, right sides up, on the right side of the paper so the edges extend beyond the edges of the marked shape. Pin the fabric for shape 2, right sides down, on top of shape 1, with edges even. From the paper side, sew with small close stitches along the seam that separates shapes 1 and 2.

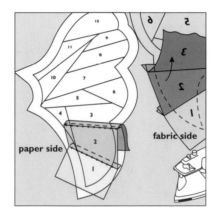

With tracing paper on top, sew along marked line. Lift and press fabrics on front.

Your stitches should be small enough to perforate the paper for easy removal when all the sewing is done. The paper must not tear away as it is being sewn.

3. Lift the fabric for shape 2, and press it to lie flat on the tracing paper, making sure that all of shape 2 is covered. Reduce the fabric along the next edge, between shapes 2 and 3, so the seam allowance extends only ¼″ beyond the marked line. Position, sew, and trim the next fabric strip, and continue to sew in sequence until the wing is complete.

4. Remove the paper from the back, leaving the fabric you have created for the wing. Follow Steps 1–4 from Workshop 6 (page 67).

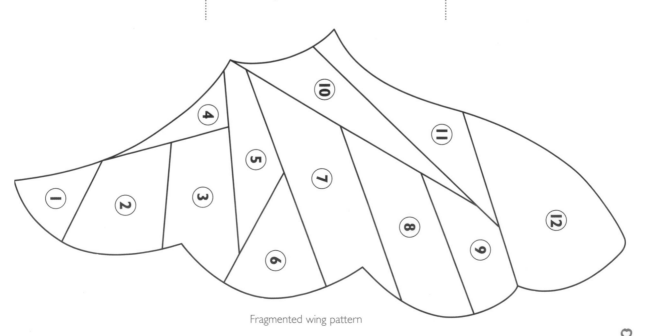

Fragmented wing pattern

Freda's Butterfly Quilt, 54″ × 78″, Freda Dodd, Connah's Quay, Flintshire, Wales, 2000.
Hand reverse appliqué and hand quilting

Gwyneth's Butterfly, 16" × 16", Gwyneth Thomas, Gresford, Flintshire, Wales 2004. Machine reverse appliqué and machine quilting

Valerie's Butterfly, 18" × 18", Valerie Frazer, Hartley Wintney, Hampshire, England 2000. Hand appliqué and reverse appliqué and hand quilting

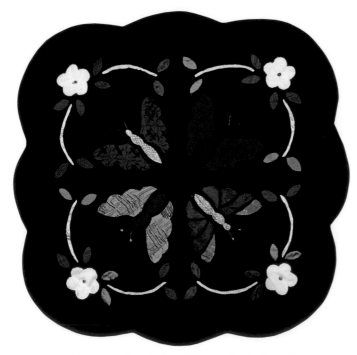

Ring Around the Butterflies, 30" × 30", Alexis Cowie, Barnt Green, Birmingham, England, 2004. Hand reverse appliqué and hand quilting

Positive and Negative Butterflies, 24" × 24", Dilys Fronks, 2004. Each foreground square was constructed with two large triangles, one light and one dark. These fabrics were reversed in the background to give a totally different effect

Template-Free Method by Machine
Reverse Appliqué Using Fusible Web

In this workshop, you will use a fusible layer to transfer the traced master pattern onto the wrong side of the foreground fabric. The fusible web stiffens the fabric and prevents fraying, so you can carefully cut out the pattern before fusing the foreground and background layers for sewing. Backing and batting layers are added so the appliqué stitch is also the quilting stitch.

FABRIC REQUIREMENTS

BACKGROUND
8″ × 8″ floral fabric

FOREGROUND
9″ × 9″ dark fabric

FUSIBLE WEB
6″ × 6″

BACKING FABRIC
11″ × 11″

BATTING
11″ × 11″

OTHER SUPPLIES

SEWING MACHINE

MACHINE THREAD that closely matches foreground fabric

DRESSMAKER'S CARBON PAPER

BALLPOINT PEN

BASIC SEWING SUPPLIES (see page 12)

PREPARATION

Transfer the pattern onto the foreground with fusible web. Trace the master pattern so it is centered on the paper side of the fusible web. Tick the pattern shapes (holes) that are to be cut away. A strip of the fusible web should extend approximately ½″ beyond the outer edges of the marked pattern.

Borders of fusible web wider than ½″ around the edges of the marked pattern are wasteful and make the fabric stiff and unyielding.

Find the center of the foreground fabric by gently finger-pressing. Place the foreground on the ironing board, with the wrong side up. Center the fusible web on top of the foreground fabric with the paper side up. Press very carefully, following the manufacturer's instructions. You only have one attempt to get it right! Let it cool.

Use small, sharp scissors to carefully trim the pattern shapes (ticked) to be discarded, leaving the pattern intact, like a stencil. Do not remove the paper until you are ready to sew.

1. **Place the background fabric behind the foreground shapes.** Place the background fabric, right side up, on the ironing board. Carefully remove the paper backing and place the fused side of the foreground fabric so it is centered on top of the background fabric. Make sure the fabric grains match and both fabrics lie flat. Carefully press and lift the iron from the center to the edges to fuse the fabrics together.

2. **Trim the background shapes.** When the fabrics have cooled, from wrong side trim the excess background fabric that lies outside the edge of the fused pattern.

Where the edge lines are straight, the excess background fabric can be folded and creased with the iron. Use the scissors flat to carefully cut along the pressed seams.

3. **Baste the shapes.** Place the prepared foreground fabric on top of the squares of batting and backing to make a batting sandwich. Pin baste the layers together in preparation for machine stitching.

4. **Machine appliqué the edges of the shapes.** Using small, controlled zigzag stitches (see page 18) and a thread that matches the foreground fabric, sew around the fused edges of the holes to appliqué and quilt at the same time. Add any other quilting lines or textures. The sample is echo quilted with a variegated thread and a decorative stitch.

Trim the excess batting and backing to the edges of the foreground square to complete.

Press fusible, marked with the pattern, onto wrong side of fabric.

Trim shapes.

Remove paper from fusible; carefully press to fuse fabrics together.

On wrong side, trim excess fabric to the fused edge.

Gwenda's Love Spoon, 9″ × 10″, Gwenda
Taylor, Blaenau Ffestiniog, Gwynedd, Wales,
2004. Hand reverse appliqué and hand quilting

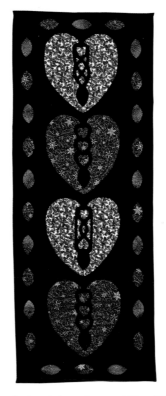

A Rainbow of Love Spoons, 9½″ × 36″,
Dilys Fronks, 2003. Machine reverse appliqué and
machine quilting with a decorative stitch

Barbara's Love Spoons, 12″ × 40″,
Barbara Lane, Thelwall, Cheshire, England
2004. Hand reverse appliqué and hand quilting

Ten Love Spoons, Dilys Fronks, 2004. I made this for an exhibition to celebrate the tenth anniversary of the Quilt Association at the Minerva Centre in Llanidloes, Powys. Machine reverse appliqué and machine quilting

BIBLIOGRAPHY

All About Quilting From A to Z, C&T Publishing: Lafayette, CA, 2002

Love Spoons From Wales, Emeralda: Cardiff, UK, 1973

Seward, Linda, *Patchwork, Appliqué, and Quilting*, Mitchell Beazley, London England,1987

Sienkiewicz, Elly, *Appliqué 12 Easy Ways*, C&T Publishing: Lafayette, CA, 1991

Index

AUTHOR'S POSTSCRIPT

As an author, I was once asked what system I used to store my fabrics. "System?," I thought; "I need a system?" This got me thinking about what I actually did with my fabrics. On careful reflection, I reckoned that I follow the "Hide and Seek" system! Like every quilter, I adore fabrics; the more the better, as far as I am concerned. I estimate my needs, double them, and add a bit more for good measure. I aspire to wire trays and a rainbow filing system, but, in reality, I bring fabrics home, give them their due fondle, and put them down wherever I can find space in my workshop (once called "Momma's Playroom" by an American visitor as she sped toward it, leaving skid marks on my carpet!). It isn't my intention to hide my fabrics, but, when I need them, I certainly have to seek them out!

I go now to unearth fabrics for a fresh creative journey, in the hope that you have enjoyed this floral pathway that we have traveled together.

Great Titles from C&T PUBLISHING

views
QUILTS INSPIRED BY WROUGHT-IRON DESIGNS
DILYS A. FRONKS

Art Glass Quilts
New Subtractive Appliqué Technique
JULIE HIROTA

Becky Goldsmith & Linda Jenkins
Curl-Up quilts
Flannel Appliqué & More from Piece O' Cake Designs

LAUREL BURCH QUILTS
KINDRED CREATURES
12 Projects for Appliqué and Embellishment

Reverse Appliqué WITH NO BRAKEZ
Jan Mullen

WONDERFULLY Whimsical Quilts
10 Playful Projects to Make You Smile
CAROL BURNISTON

Available at your local retailer or
www.ctpub.com or 800.284.1114